Let's Keep in Touch

Follow Us

Online

Visit US at

www.EffortlessMath.com

 https://www.facebook.com/Effortlessmath

Call

https://goo.gl/2B6qWW

1-469-230-3605

Online Math Lessons

It's easy! Here's how it works.

1- Request a FREE introductory session.

2- Meet a Math tutor online.

3- Start Learning Math in Minutes.

Send Email to: **info@EffortlessMath.com**

Or Call: **+1-469-230-3605**

www.EffortlessMath.com

... So Much More Online!

- **FREE Math lessons**

- **More Math learning books!**

- **Online Math Tutors**

3rd Grade Georgia Milestones Assessment System Math Workbook 2018

The Most Comprehensive Review for the Math Section of the GMAS TEST

By

Reza Nazari

& Ava Ross

All inquiries should be addressed to:

info@effortlessMath.com

www.EffortlessMath.com

ISBN-13: 978-1986288842

ISBN-10: 1986288846

Published by: Effortless Math Education

www.EffortlessMath.com

Description

Effortless Math GMAS Workbook provides students with the confidence and math skills they need to succeed on the Georgia Milestones Assessment System Math, providing a solid foundation of basic Math topics with abundant exercises for each topic. It is designed to address the needs of GMAS test takers who must have a working knowledge of basic Math.

This comprehensive workbook with over 1,500 sample questions and 2 complete 3rd Grade GMAS tests is all your student needs to fully prepare for the GMAS Math. It will help your student learns everything they need to ace the math section of the GMAS.

There are more than 1,500 Math problems with answers in this book.
Effortless Math unique study program provides your student with an in–depth focus on the math portion of the exam, helping them master the math skills that students find the most troublesome.
This workbook contains most common sample questions that are most likely to appear in the mathematics section of the GMAS.

Inside the pages of this comprehensive workbook, students can learn basic math operations in a structured manner with a complete study program to help them understand essential math skills. It also has many exciting features, including:

- Dynamic design and easy–to–follow activities
- A fun, interactive and concrete learning process
- Targeted, skill–building practices
- Fun exercises that build confidence
- Math topics are grouped by category, so the students can focus on the topics they struggle on
- All solutions for the exercises are included, so you will always find the answers
- 2 Complete GMAS Math Practice Tests that reflect the format and question types on GMAS

Effortless Math GMAS Workbook is an incredibly useful tool for those who want to review all topics being covered on the GMAS test. It efficiently and effectively reinforces learning outcomes through engaging questions and repeated practice, helping students to quickly master basic Math skills.

About the Author

Reza Nazari is the author of more than 100 Math learning books including:
– **Math for Super Smart Students:** Fifth Graders and Older by Reza Nazari
– **Math and Critical Thinking Challenges:** For the Middle and High School Student
– **Effortless Math Education Workbooks**

Reza is also an experienced Math instructor and a test–prep expert who has been tutoring students since 2008. Reza is the founder of Effortless Math Education, a tutoring company that has helped many students raise their Math knowledge—and succeed in their studies. Reza provides an individualized custom learning plan and the personalized attention that makes a difference in how students view math.

You can contact Reza via email at:
Reza@EffortlessMath.com

Find Reza's professional profile at:
goo.gl/zoC9rJ

Contents

Repeating pattern

Circle the picture that comes next in each picture pattern.

1)

2)

3)

4)

5)

6)

7)

8)

Growing Patterns

Draw the picture that comes next in each growing pattern.

1)

2)

3)

4)

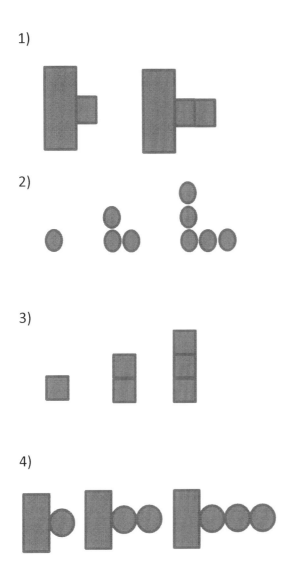

5)

6)

7)

8)

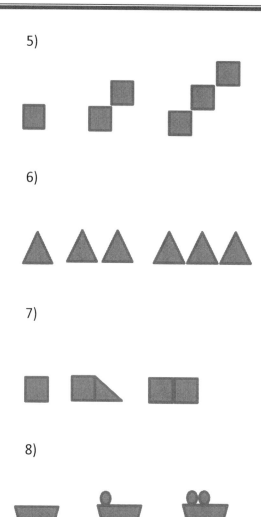

Adding Two–Digit Numbers

Find each sum.

1.
$$
\begin{array}{r}
50 \\
+\ 18 \\
\hline
\end{array}
$$

2.
$$
\begin{array}{r}
32 \\
+\ 14 \\
\hline
\end{array}
$$

3.
$$
\begin{array}{r}
45 \\
+\ 16 \\
\hline
\end{array}
$$

4.
$$
\begin{array}{r}
12 \\
+\ 12 \\
\hline
\end{array}
$$

5.
$$
\begin{array}{r}
43 \\
+\ 30 \\
\hline
\end{array}
$$

6.
$$
\begin{array}{r}
34 \\
+\ 15 \\
\hline
\end{array}
$$

7.
$$
\begin{array}{r}
89 \\
+\ 7 \\
\hline
\end{array}
$$

8.
$$
\begin{array}{r}
63 \\
+\ 12 \\
\hline
\end{array}
$$

9.
$$
\begin{array}{r}
90 \\
+\ 10 \\
\hline
\end{array}
$$

Add.

10. $14 + 14 =$ ——

11. $16 + 18 =$ ——

12. $56 + 17 =$ ——

13. $89 + 20 =$ ——

14. $34 + 20 =$ ——

15. $53 + 30 =$ ——

16. $95 + 15 =$ ——

17. $85 + 10 =$ ——

18. $70 + 10 =$ ——

19. $20 + 10 =$ ——

20. $15 + 15 =$ ——

21. $39 + 19 =$ ——

22. $48 + 12 =$ ——

23. $29 + 34 =$ ——

Subtracting Two–Digit Numbers

Find each difference.

1.
$$\begin{array}{r} 32 \\ -15 \\ \hline \end{array}$$

2.
$$\begin{array}{r} 40 \\ -12 \\ \hline \end{array}$$

3.
$$\begin{array}{r} 67 \\ -17 \\ \hline \end{array}$$

4.
$$\begin{array}{r} 18 \\ -10 \\ \hline \end{array}$$

5.
$$\begin{array}{r} 59 \\ -16 \\ \hline \end{array}$$

6.
$$\begin{array}{r} 89 \\ -20 \\ \hline \end{array}$$

7.
$$\begin{array}{r} 78 \\ -21 \\ \hline \end{array}$$

8.
$$\begin{array}{r} 66 \\ -15 \\ \hline \end{array}$$

9.
$$\begin{array}{r} 87 \\ -45 \\ \hline \end{array}$$

Subtract.

10. $75 - 25 =$ ——

11. $47 - 37 =$ ——

12. $92 - 16 =$ ——

13. $78 - 37 =$ ——

14. $45 - 20 =$ ——

15. $66 - 23 =$ ——

16. $99 - 68 =$ ——

17. $95 - 40 =$ ——

18. $83 - 51 =$ ——

19. $61 - 48 =$ ——

20. $42 - 15 =$ ——

21. $84 - 67 =$ ——

22. $58 - 22 =$ ——

23. $63 - 23 =$ ——

Adding Three–Digit Numbers

Find each sum.

1.
$$\begin{array}{r} 234 \\ +\ 56 \\ \hline \end{array}$$

2.
$$\begin{array}{r} 523 \\ +\ 134 \\ \hline \end{array}$$

3.
$$\begin{array}{r} 345 \\ +\ 167 \\ \hline \end{array}$$

4.
$$\begin{array}{r} 460 \\ +\ 120 \\ \hline \end{array}$$

5.
$$\begin{array}{r} 432 \\ +\ 430 \\ \hline \end{array}$$

6.
$$\begin{array}{r} 235 \\ +\ 150 \\ \hline \end{array}$$

7.
$$\begin{array}{r} 789 \\ +\ 57 \\ \hline \end{array}$$

8.
$$\begin{array}{r} 863 \\ +\ 340 \\ \hline \end{array}$$

9.
$$\begin{array}{r} 956 \\ +\ 89 \\ \hline \end{array}$$

Add the numbers together.

10. 230 + 45 = ——   17. 156 + 25 = —

11. 450 + 78 = ——   18. 567 + 234 = —

12. 245 + 125 = ——   19. 678 + 456 = ——

13. 980 + 23 = ——   20. 145 + 56 = ——

14. 678 + 23 = ——   21. 689 + 76 = ——

15. 360 + 349 = ——   22. 560 + 30 = ——

16. 567 + 12 = ——   23. 256 + 140 = ——

Calendars

September						
Sun	Mon	Tue	Wed	Thu	Fri	Sat
					1	2
3	4	5	6	7	8	9
10	11	12	13	14	15	16
17	18	19	20	21	22	23
24	25	26	27	28	29	30

1. How many Fridays are in the calendar?

   _____

2. What is the day on the 1st of September?

   _____

3. What is the date in the second Monday of the month?

May						
Sun	Mon	Tue	Wed	Thu	Fri	Sat
	1	2	3	4	5	6
7	8	9	10	11 My father's birthday	12	13
14 Mather's day	15	16	17	18	19	20
21	22	23	24	25	26	27
28	29 Memorial Day	30	31			

4. What is the date of Mother's Day on the calendar? _____

5. What is the date of Memorial Day on the calendar? _____

6. What is the date of my father's birthday on calendar? _____

7. What is the day on 15th of May? _____

8. How many days are in May? _____

Adding Hundreds

1. $200 + 200 =$ ——

2. $300 + 200 =$ ——

3. $500 + 200 =$ ——

4. $900 + 100 =$ ——

5. $100 + 700 =$ ——

6. $500 + 100 =$ ——

7. $200 + 800 =$ ——

8. $800 + 100 =$ —

9. $700 + 100 =$ —

10. $100 + 300 =$ ——

11. $500 + 500 =$ ——

12. $400 + 400 =$ ——

13. $300 + 400 =$ ——

14. $500 + 300 =$ ——

15. If there are 600 balls in a box and Jackson puts 500 more balls inside, how many balls are in the box?

_____ balls

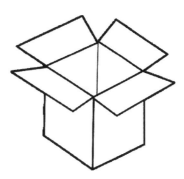

16.
$$
\begin{array}{r}
100 \\
+100 \\
\hline
\end{array}
$$

17.
$$
\begin{array}{r}
400 \\
+300 \\
\hline
\end{array}
$$

18.
$$
\begin{array}{r}
600 \\
+300 \\
\hline
\end{array}
$$

19.
$$
\begin{array}{r}
500 \\
+100 \\
\hline
\end{array}
$$

20.
$$
\begin{array}{r}
200 \\
+200 \\
\hline
\end{array}
$$

21.
$$
\begin{array}{r}
300 \\
+200 \\
\hline
\end{array}
$$

22.
$$
\begin{array}{r}
800 \\
+100 \\
\hline
\end{array}
$$

23.
$$
\begin{array}{r}
400 \\
+200 \\
\hline
\end{array}
$$

24.
$$
\begin{array}{r}
400 \\
+500 \\
\hline
\end{array}
$$

25.
$$
\begin{array}{r}
500 \\
+300 \\
\hline
\end{array}
$$

26.
$$
\begin{array}{r}
900 \\
+400 \\
\hline
\end{array}
$$

27.
$$
\begin{array}{r}
600 \\
+600 \\
\hline
\end{array}
$$

28. Mila starts with 800 stamps. She buys 300 more. How many stamps does Mila have now?

_____ stamps

Round 3–Digit Numbers

Round these numbers to the nearest hundred.

1. 125 _____   2. 756 _____

3. 378 _____   4. 289 _____

5. 320 _____   6. 765 _____

7. 934 _____   8. 421 _____

9. 567 _____   10. 312 _____

11. 923 _____   12. 480 _____

13. 276 _____   14. 756 _____

15. 476 _____   16. 408 _____

17. 255 _____   18. 176 _____

19. 392 _____   20. 359 _____

Round these numbers to the nearest thousand.

21. 2345 _____   22. 6560 _____

23. 5250 _____   24. 1570 _____

25. 2870 _____   26. 7550 _____

27. 4340 _____   28. 2220 _____

29. 5110 _____   30. 8670 _____

31. 3218 _____   32. 4320 _____

33. 2160 _____   34. 6777 _____

35. 1789 _____   36. 2930 _____

37. 6789 _____   38. 1324 _____

39. 8356 _____   40. 7654 _____

Adding 4–Digit Numbers

Add the numbers.

1.
$$\begin{array}{r} 2,000 \\ +1,500 \\ \hline \end{array}$$

2.
$$\begin{array}{r} 1,344 \\ +1,556 \\ \hline \end{array}$$

3.
$$\begin{array}{r} 2,333 \\ +1,211 \\ \hline \end{array}$$

4.
$$\begin{array}{r} 3,221 \\ +2,345 \\ \hline \end{array}$$

5.
$$\begin{array}{r} 1,906 \\ +1,178 \\ \hline \end{array}$$

6.
$$\begin{array}{r} 3,150 \\ +3,741 \\ \hline \end{array}$$

7.
$$\begin{array}{r} 4,623 \\ +3,867 \\ \hline \end{array}$$

8.
$$\begin{array}{r} 3,599 \\ +2,978 \\ \hline \end{array}$$

9.
$$
\begin{array}{r}
6,998 \\
+1,456 \\
\hline

\end{array}
$$

10.
$$
\begin{array}{r}
2,560 \\
+2,210 \\
\hline

\end{array}
$$

11.
$$
\begin{array}{r}
5,590 \\
+3,191 \\
\hline

\end{array}
$$

12.
$$
\begin{array}{r}
8,845 \\
+1,230 \\
\hline

\end{array}
$$

13.
$$
\begin{array}{r}
1,798 \\
+1,500 \\
\hline

\end{array}
$$

14.
$$
\begin{array}{r}
2,293 \\
+4,222 \\
\hline

\end{array}
$$

15.
$$
\begin{array}{r}
4,791 \\
+1,500 \\
\hline

\end{array}
$$

16.
$$
\begin{array}{r}
6,418 \\
+2,811 \\
\hline

\end{array}
$$

17.
$$
\begin{array}{r}
3,467 \\
+1,808 \\
\hline

\end{array}
$$

18.
$$
\begin{array}{r}
3,210 \\
+4,211 \\
\hline

\end{array}
$$

Subtracting 4–Digit Numbers

Subtract the numbers.

1.
$$\begin{array}{r} 5,600 \\ -3,500 \\ \hline \end{array}$$

2.
$$\begin{array}{r} 6,700 \\ -1,200 \\ \hline \end{array}$$

3.
$$\begin{array}{r} 3,456 \\ -2,342 \\ \hline \end{array}$$

4.
$$\begin{array}{r} 5,897 \\ -1,234 \\ \hline \end{array}$$

5.
$$\begin{array}{r} 9,800 \\ -5,255 \\ \hline \end{array}$$

6.
$$\begin{array}{r} 6,340 \\ -2,500 \\ \hline \end{array}$$

7.
$$\begin{array}{r} 4,235 \\ -2,450 \\ \hline \end{array}$$

8.
$$\begin{array}{r} 7,340 \\ -5,210 \\ \hline \end{array}$$

9.
$$\begin{array}{r} 5{,}234 \\ -2{,}321 \\ \hline \\ \hline \end{array}$$

10.
$$\begin{array}{r} 3{,}121 \\ -1{,}456 \\ \hline \\ \hline \end{array}$$

11.
$$\begin{array}{r} 6{,}100 \\ -2{,}500 \\ \hline \\ \hline \end{array}$$

12.
$$\begin{array}{r} 6{,}500 \\ -5{,}456 \\ \hline \\ \hline \end{array}$$

13.
$$\begin{array}{r} 5{,}355 \\ -2{,}333 \\ \hline \\ \hline \end{array}$$

14.
$$\begin{array}{r} 7{,}120 \\ -4{,}000 \\ \hline \\ \hline \end{array}$$

15.
$$\begin{array}{r} 8{,}560 \\ -3{,}945 \\ \hline \\ \hline \end{array}$$

16.
$$\begin{array}{r} 9{,}257 \\ -7{,}910 \\ \hline \\ \hline \end{array}$$

17.
$$\begin{array}{r} 9{,}610 \\ -8{,}250 \\ \hline \\ \hline \end{array}$$

18.
$$\begin{array}{r} 5{,}311 \\ -3{,}100 \\ \hline \\ \hline \end{array}$$

Estimate Sums

Estimate the sum by rounding each added to the nearest ten.

1) 55 + 9

2) 13 + 74

3) 83 + 7

4) 32 + 37

5) 13 + 74

6) 34 + 11

7) 39 + 77

8) 25 + 4

9) 61 + 73

10) 64 + 59

11) 14 + 68

12) 82 + 12

13) 43 + 66

19) 78 + 74

14) 45 + 65

20) 39 + 27

15) 553 + 232

21) 91 + 68

16) 52 + 67

22) 48 + 81

17) 96 + 94

23) 14 + 96

18) 29 + 89

24) 52 + 59

Estimate Differences

Estimate the difference by rounding each number to the nearest ten.

1) $46 - 11$

2) $23 + 16$

3) $68 + 36$

4) $22 - 13$

5) $59 + 36$

6) $34 - 11$

7) $67 - 37$

8) $38 - 19$

9) $84 - 38$

10) $68 - 48$

11) $58 - 16$

12) $72 - 27$

13) $63 - 33$

14) $49 - 32$

15) $94 + 63$

16) $55 - 32$

17) $87 - 74$

18) $32 - 11$

19) $46 - 39$

20) $99 - 36$

21) $94 - 78$

22) $75 - 23$

23) $99 - 19$

24) $86 - 43$

Estimate Products

Estimate the products.

1) 27×18

2) 13×17

3) 22×25

4) 43×19

5) 68×23

6) 36×91

7) 53×92

8) 18×38

9) 21×14

10) 83×42

11) 51×32

12) 68×12

13) 47×23

19) 41×37

14) 71×58

20) 54×93

15) 54×89

21) 89×72

16) 37×72

22) 77×22

17) 36×93

23) 53×13

18) 32×29

24) 98×63

Fractions

Color $\frac{1}{2}$ of each shape.

1.

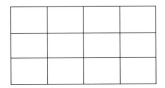

2.

3.

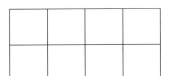

4.

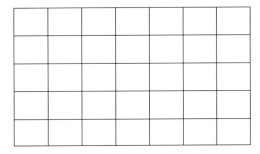

Shade the lower parts to make the fractions equivalent, then write the fractions.

5.

6.

7.

8.

Fractions of a Number

1) Find $\frac{1}{2}$ of 40

2) Find $\frac{2}{3}$ of 90

3) Find $\frac{1}{2}$ of 50

4) Find $\frac{3}{4}$ of 16

5) Find $\frac{1}{5}$ of 10

6) Find $\frac{3}{5}$ of 20

7) Find $\frac{1}{3}$ of 27

8) Find $\frac{2}{5}$ of 50

9) Find $\frac{1}{6}$ of 12

10) Find $\frac{3}{7}$ of 21

11) Find $\frac{5}{8}$ of 40

16) Find $\frac{3}{8}$ of 144

12) Find $\frac{4}{7}$ of 49

17) Find $\frac{5}{8}$ of 480

13) Find $\frac{1}{8}$ of 80

18) Find $\frac{4}{10}$ of 320

14) Find $\frac{1}{3}$ of 9

19) Find $\frac{2}{3}$ of 42

15) Find $\frac{3}{4}$ of 132

20) Find $\frac{2}{10}$ of 120

Order Fractions

Order the fractions from greatest to latest.

1) $\frac{1}{2}, \frac{2}{3}, \frac{1}{4}$

2) $\frac{1}{10}, \frac{7}{10}, \frac{1}{2}$

3) $\frac{3}{10}, \frac{5}{8}, \frac{1}{10}$

4) $\frac{3}{8}, \frac{3}{4}, \frac{4}{7}$

5) $\frac{1}{3}, \frac{3}{8}, \frac{7}{10}$

6) $\frac{1}{8}, \frac{1}{2}, \frac{3}{8}$

7) $\frac{1}{2}, \frac{1}{5}, \frac{2}{5}$

8) $\frac{3}{8}, \frac{9}{8}, \frac{5}{8}$

9) $\frac{4}{5}, \frac{2}{5}, \frac{3}{5}$

10) $\frac{8}{3}, \frac{1}{3}, \frac{5}{3}$

Order the fractions from latest to greatest.

1) $\dfrac{7}{3}, \dfrac{5}{3}, \dfrac{8}{3}$

6) $\dfrac{9}{2}, \dfrac{5}{2}, \dfrac{3}{2}$

2) $\dfrac{5}{9}, \dfrac{8}{9}, \dfrac{4}{9}$

7) $\dfrac{11}{3}, \dfrac{2}{3}, \dfrac{8}{3}$

3) $\dfrac{5}{8}, \dfrac{3}{8}, \dfrac{1}{8}$

8) $\dfrac{18}{5}, \dfrac{22}{5}, \dfrac{19}{5}$

4) $\dfrac{1}{4}, \dfrac{3}{4}, \dfrac{2}{4}$

9) $\dfrac{4}{13}, \dfrac{8}{13}, \dfrac{12}{13}$

5) $\dfrac{3}{7}, \dfrac{5}{7}, \dfrac{1}{7}$

10) $\dfrac{3}{20}, \dfrac{18}{20}, \dfrac{11}{20}$

Value of "x"

What is the value of x in the following equations?

1. $x + 6 = 8$

    _____

2. $3 + 1 + x = 6$

    _____

3. $4 + x = 10$

    _____

4. $x + 9 + 3 = 15$

    _____

5. $4 + x = 12$

    _____

6. $9 + x = 16$

    _____

7. $8 + x + 5 = 18$

    _____

8. $6 + x = 14$

    _____

9. $x + 12 = 13$

    _____

10. $15 + 5 = x$

    _____

11. $16 + x + 4 = 24$

    _____

12. $x + 12 + 5 = 25$

    _____

13. $5 + 9 = x$

19. $14 + x = 30$

_____

_____

14. $x + 12 + 24 = 40$

20. $19 + x + 29 = 50$

_____

_____

15. $20 + x + 12 = 36$

21. $x + 25 = 60$

_____

_____

16. $13 + 19 = x$

22. $34 + 9 + x = 47$

_____

_____

17. $10 + 12 + 5 = x$

23. $21 + x + 9 = 35$

_____

_____

18. $13 + 12 + x = 30$

24. $12 + 35 = x$

_____

_____

Comparing Numbers

Use > = < in the box.

1. 35 ☐ 67

2. 89 ☐ 56

3. 56 ☐ 35

4. 27 ☐ 56

5. 34 ☐ 34

6. 28 ☐ 45

7. 89 ☐ 67

8. 90 ☐ 56

9. 94 ☐ 98

10. 48 ☐ 23

11. 24 ☐ 54

12. 89 ☐ 89

13. 50 ☐ 30

14. 20 ☐ 20

Use less than, equal to or greater than to compare following numbers.

15. 23 _____ 34

16. 89 _____ 98

17. 45 _____ 25

18. 34 _____ 32

19. 91 _____ 91

20. 57 _____ 55

21. 85 _____ 78

22. 56 _____ 43

23. 34 _____ 34

24. 92 _____ 98

25. 38 _____ 46

26. 67 _____ 58

27. 88 _____ 69

28. 23 _____ 34

Adding Decimal Numbers

Add decimals.

1.
$$
\begin{array}{r}
5.5 \\
+\ 1.5 \\
\hline
\end{array}
$$

2.
$$
\begin{array}{r}
1.5 \\
+\ 1.5 \\
\hline
\end{array}
$$

3.
$$
\begin{array}{r}
9.3 \\
+\ 2.5 \\
\hline
\end{array}
$$

4.
$$
\begin{array}{r}
8.6 \\
+\ 1.7 \\
\hline
\end{array}
$$

5.
$$
\begin{array}{r}
6.2 \\
+\ 4.5 \\
\hline
\end{array}
$$

6.
$$
\begin{array}{r}
3.8 \\
+\ 4.1 \\
\hline
\end{array}
$$

7.
$$
\begin{array}{r}
7.9 \\
+\ 7.2 \\
\hline
\end{array}
$$

8.
$$
\begin{array}{r}
4.6 \\
+\ 2.3 \\
\hline
\end{array}
$$

9.
$$
\begin{array}{r}
8.5 \\
+\ 9.4 \\
\hline
\end{array}
$$

10.
$$\begin{array}{r} 6.1 \\ + 2.2 \\ \hline \end{array}$$

11.
$$\begin{array}{r} 4.9 \\ + 3.7 \\ \hline \end{array}$$

12.
$$\begin{array}{r} 6.3 \\ + 6.5 \\ \hline \end{array}$$

13.
$$\begin{array}{r} 6.5 \\ + 4.2 \\ \hline \end{array}$$

14.
$$\begin{array}{r} 3.3 \\ + 8.1 \\ \hline \end{array}$$

15.
$$\begin{array}{r} 4.5 \\ + 4.5 \\ \hline \end{array}$$

16.
$$\begin{array}{r} 2.3 \\ + 2.9 \\ \hline \end{array}$$

17.
$$\begin{array}{r} 4.7 \\ + 3.2 \\ \hline \end{array}$$

18.
$$\begin{array}{r} 5.1 \\ + 3.2 \\ \hline \end{array}$$

Positions

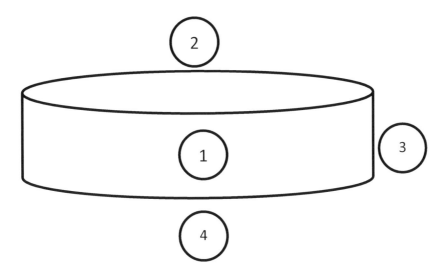

What is the position of the balls? Circle the answer.

1.  under   inside   top   at the side

2. (2)   under   inside   top   at the side

3. (3)   under   inside   top   at the side

4. (4)   under   inside   top   at the side

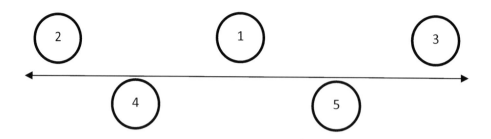

5. ③   Left   Middle   Right

6. ①   Left   Middle   Right

7. ②   Left   Middle   Right

8. ⑤   Left   Middle   Right

9. ④   Left   Middle   Right

Read Clocks

Write the time below each clock.

1)

_____

2)

_____

3)

_____

4)

_____

5)

_____

5)

_____

Draw the hands on the clock face.

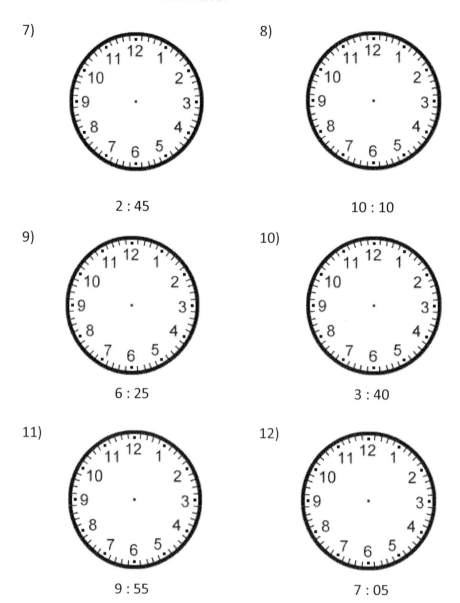

7)

2 : 45

8)

10 : 10

9)

6 : 25

10)

3 : 40

11)

9 : 55

12)

7 : 05

Electronic Clock

What time is it? Write the time in words in front of each.

1. 2 : 30   _____

2. 3 : 15   _____

3. 5 : 45   _____

4. 9 : 20   _____

5. 10 : 5   _____

6. 12 : 50   _____

7. 10 : 25   _____

8. 3 : 23   _____

9. 11 : 57   _____

10. 2 : 12   _____

11. 1 : 02   _____

12. 8 : 35   _____

13. 6 : 46
                               _____

Multiplication by 0, 1, 2 , and 3

Write the answers.

1. $9 \times 2 = $ ___

2. $7 \times 4 = $ ___

3. $10 \times 3 = $ ___

4. $8 \times 0 = $ ___

5. $6 \times 2 = $ ___

6. $5 \times 3 = $ ___

7. $9 \times 8 = $ ___

8. $15 \times 2 = $ ___

9. $11 \times 2 = $ ___

10. $12 \times 3 = $ ___

11. Mommy bought 3 egg cartons, and each had 13 eggs. How many eggs did Mommy buy?

_____

Find Each Missing Number.

12. $3 \times \underline{\hspace{0.6cm}} = 27$ 13. $2 \times \underline{\hspace{0.6cm}} = 16$

14. $6 \times \underline{\hspace{0.6cm}} = 12$ 15. $6 \times \underline{\hspace{0.6cm}} = 18$

16. $7 \times 3 = \underline{\hspace{0.6cm}}$ 17. $\underline{\hspace{0.6cm}} \times 2 = 6$

18. $\underline{\hspace{0.6cm}} \times 2 = 8$ 19. $\underline{\hspace{0.6cm}} \times 3 = 6$

20. $\underline{\hspace{0.6cm}} \times 5 = 15$ 21. $3 \times 10 = \underline{\hspace{0.6cm}}$

22. $3 \times \underline{\hspace{0.6cm}} = 0$ 23. $2 \times \underline{\hspace{0.6cm}} = 18$

24. $2 \times \underline{\hspace{0.6cm}} = 2$ 25. $\underline{\hspace{0.6cm}} \times 3 = 9$

26. Mr. Smith usually eats three meals a day. How many

meals does he eat in a week?

_____

Multiplication by 4, 5, 6

Write the answers.

1. $10 \times 4 =$ ___

2. $8 \times 6 =$ ___

3. $9 \times 5 =$ ___

4. $7 \times 4 =$ ___

5. $8 \times 4 =$ ___

6. $9 \times 6 =$ ___

7. $6 \times 6 =$ ___

8. $12 \times 7 =$ ___

9. $9 \times 8 =$ ___

10. $11 \times 6 =$ ___

11. Ryan ordered eight pizzas and sliced them into six pieces each. How many pieces of pizza were there?

12. Match the answers to the questions.

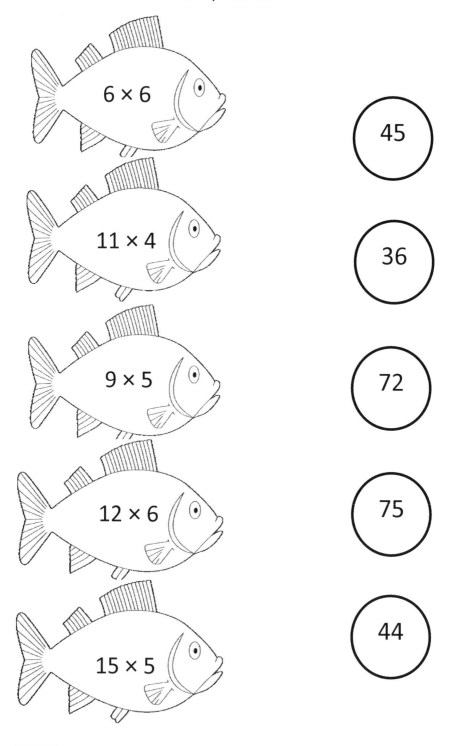

6×6

11×4

9×5

12×6

15×5

45

36

72

75

44

Multiplication by 7, 8, 9

Write the answers.

1. $7 \times 7 =$ ___

2. $9 \times 8 =$ ___

3. $5 \times 9 =$ ___

4. $10 \times 7 =$ ___

5. $11 \times 8 =$ ___

6. $7 \times 9 =$ ___

7. $12 \times 9 =$ ___

8. $8 \times 8 =$ ___

9. $9 \times 9 =$ ___

10. $11 \times 7 =$ ___

11. There are 12 bananas in each box. How many bananas are in 8 boxes? _____

12. Each child has 8 apples. If there are 7 children, how many apples are there in total? _____

Find each missing number.

13. ___ × 7 = 0

14. ___ × 8 = 72

15. 8 × ___ = 64

16. ___ × 9 = 63

17. 9 × ___ = 81

18. 8 × ___ = 40

19. ___ × 7 = 70

20. 9 × ___ = 45

21. 8 × 1 = ___

22. ___ × 8 = 16

23. 7 × ___ = 14

24. 7 × 8 = ___

25. 9 × ___ = 9

26. 9 × 8 = ___

27. 8 × 2 = ___

28. 8 × ___ = 80

29. 7 × ___ = 63

30. 9 × 9 = ___

31. There are 9 Skittles in each box. How many Skittles are in 8 boxes?

_____ skittles

Multiplication by 10, 11, 12

Write the answers.

1. 6 × 11 = ___   2. 8 × 12= ___

3. 6 × 10 = ___   4. 3 × 11 = ___

5. 9 × 12 = ___   6. 4 × 10 = ___

7. 11 × 8 = ___   8. 12 × 5 = ___

9. 10 × 9 = ___   10. 12 × 12 = ___

11. 8 × 10 = ___   12. 12 × 10 = ___

13. Each child has 12 pencils. If there are 11 children, how

    many pens are there in total?

    _____ pencils

Find Each Missing Number.

14. $12 \times$ ____ $= 96$

15. $10 \times 7 =$ ____

16. $12 \times 3 =$ ____

17. ____ $\times 12 = 72$

18. $10 \times$ ____ $= 90$

19. $12 \times 9 =$ ____

20. $12 \times 6 =$ ____

21. $10 \times$ ____ $= 10$

22. ____ $\times 11 = 88$

23. $12 \times$ ____ $= 12$

24. ____ $\times 11 = 77$

25. $11 \times 6 =$ ____

26. ____ $\times 12 = 48$

27. $11 \times 5 =$ ____

28. Kevin has 14 boxes of cards. Each box holds 12 cards. How many cards does Kevin have?

_____ cards

29. Larry has 15 boxes of eggs. Each box holds 10 eggs. How many eggs does Larry have?

_____ eggs

Division by 0, 1, 2, 3

Find each missing number.

1. $22 \div \underline{\hspace{1cm}} = 11$

2. $24 \div 3 = \underline{\hspace{1cm}}$

3. $12 \div 2 = \underline{\hspace{1cm}}$

4. $36 \div 3 = \underline{\hspace{1cm}}$

5. $\underline{\hspace{1cm}} \div 3 = 3$

6. $10 \div 2 = \underline{\hspace{1cm}}$

7. $\underline{\hspace{1cm}} \div 3 = 4$

8. $18 \div \underline{\hspace{1cm}} = 9$

9. $\underline{\hspace{1cm}} \div 2 = 8$

10. $\underline{\hspace{1cm}} \div 3 = 6$

11. $\underline{\hspace{1cm}} \div 2 = 1$

12. $3 \div 3 = \underline{\hspace{1cm}}$

13. $6 \div \underline{\hspace{1cm}} = 3$

14. $14 \div 2 = \underline{\hspace{1cm}}$

15. $6 \div \underline{\hspace{1cm}} = 2$

16. $\underline{\hspace{1cm}} \div 3 = 7$

17. Jessica has 30 strawberries that she would like to give to her 3 friends. If she shares them equally, how many strawberries will she give to each of her friends?

_____ strawberries

Find the answers.

$9 \times 3 = 27$ $27 \div 3 = 9$

18. $4 \times 2 = \underline{}$ $\underline{} \div 2 = \underline{}$

19. $8 \times 3 = \underline{}$ $\underline{} \div 3 = \underline{}$

20. $10 \times 2 = \underline{}$ $\underline{} \div 2 = \underline{}$

21. $6 \times 3 = \underline{}$ $\underline{} \div 3 = \underline{}$

22. $12 \times 2 = \underline{}$ $\underline{} \div 2 = \underline{}$

Find the answers.

23. $\dfrac{20}{2} = \underline{}$ 24. $\dfrac{15}{3} = \underline{}$

25. $\dfrac{27}{3} = \underline{}$ 26. $\dfrac{18}{2} = \underline{}$

Division by 4, 5, 6

Find each missing number.

1. $30 \div 5 =$ ___

2. $48 \div$ ___ $= 8$

3. $60 \div$ ___ $= 12$

4. $24 \div$ ___ $= 6$

5. $30 \div 6 =$ ___

6. $20 \div 4 =$ ___

7. ___ $\div 6 = 3$

8. $72 \div$ ___ $= 12$

9. $48 \div 4 =$ ___

10. $6 \div$ ___ $= 1$

11. $60 \div$ ___ $= 10$

12. $12 \div$ ___ $= 3$

13. $36 \div$ ___ $= 9$

14. ___ $\div 6 = 7$

15. $16 \div 4 =$ ___

16. $10 \div 5 =$ ___

17. ___ $\div 5 = 4$

18. $40 \div 5 =$ ___

19. $12 \div 6 =$ ___

20. ___ $\div 6 = 9$

21. Hanna has 48 marbles that she would like to give to her 6 friends. If she shares them equally, how many marbles will she give to each?

_____ marbles

22. Match the answers to the right division.

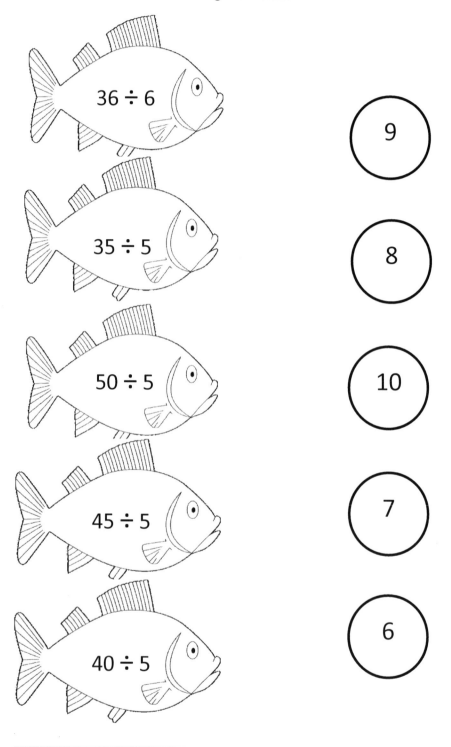

$36 \div 6$

$35 \div 5$

$50 \div 5$

$45 \div 5$

$40 \div 5$

9

8

10

7

6

Division by 7, 8, 9

Find each missing number.

1. ___ ÷ 8 = 1

2. ___ ÷ 7 = 3

3. 88 ÷ 8 = ___

4. 77 ÷ ___ = 11

5. 64 ÷ 8 = ___

6. ___ ÷ 9 = 9

7. 28 ÷ ___ = 4

8. ___ ÷ 8 = 9

9. 54 ÷ ___ = 6

10. 35 ÷ 7 = ___

11. ___ ÷ 7 = 9

12. 27 ÷ ___ = 3

13. ___ ÷ 7 = 49

14. 16 ÷ 8 = ___

15. 99 ÷ ___ = 11

16. 63 ÷ 7 = ___

17. 80 ÷ 8 = ___

18. 63 ÷ 9 = ___

19. Emily has 64 fruit juice that she would like to give to her 8 friends. If she shares them equally, how many fruit juices will she give to each? _____ fruit juice

Find the Missing Numbers.

$6 \times 7 = 42$ $42 \div 6 = 7$

20. $9 \times 4 = \underline{\ \ }$ $\underline{\ \ } \div 9 = \underline{\ \ }$

21. $7 \times 8 = \underline{\ \ }$ $\underline{\ \ } \div 7 = \underline{\ \ }$

22. $6 \times 8 = \underline{\ \ }$ $\underline{\ \ } \div 8 = \underline{\ \ }$

23. $9 \times 8 = \underline{\ \ }$ $\underline{\ \ } \div 9 = \underline{\ \ }$

24. $8 \times 5 = \underline{\ \ }$ $\underline{\ \ } \div 8 = \underline{\ \ }$

25. What multiplication fact can help you find the answer of $64 \div 8$?

$$\underline{\quad\quad} \times \underline{\quad\quad} = \underline{\quad\quad}$$

25. What multiplication fact can help you find the answer of $72 \div 9$?

$$\underline{\quad\quad} \times \underline{\quad\quad} = \underline{\quad\quad}$$

Division by 10, 11, 12

Find each missing number.

1. $10 \div \underline{\quad} = 1$

2. $48 \div 12 = \underline{\quad}$

3. $99 \div \underline{\quad} = 9$

4. $70 \div 10 = \underline{\quad}$

5. $44 \div \underline{\quad} = 4$

6. $24 \div \underline{\quad} = 2$

7. $\underline{\quad} \div 10 = 4$

8. $110 \div 11 = \underline{\quad}$

9. $12 \div \underline{\quad} = 1$

10. $90 \div \underline{\quad} = 9$

11. $\underline{\quad} \div 11 = 8$

12. $\underline{\quad} \div 12 = 11$

13. $60 \div \underline{\quad} = 6$

14. $\underline{\quad} \div 11 = 12$

15. $84 \div 12 = \underline{\quad}$

16. $80 \div 10 = \underline{\quad}$

17. $11 \div 11 = \underline{\quad}$

18. $144 \div \underline{\quad} = 12$

19. Anna has 120 books. She wants to put them in equal numbers on 12 bookshelves. How many books can she put on a bookshelf?   _____ books

20. If dividend is 99 and the quotient is 11, then what is the divisor? _____

Simplify each fraction.

21. $\dfrac{72}{12} =$ _____

22. $\dfrac{96}{12} =$ _____

23. $\dfrac{99}{11} =$ _____

24. $\dfrac{108}{12} =$ _____

25. $\dfrac{88}{11} =$ _____

26. $\dfrac{33}{11} =$ _____

27. $\dfrac{144}{12} =$ _____

28. $\dfrac{120}{12} =$ _____

29. $\dfrac{72}{12} =$ _____

30. $\dfrac{22}{11} =$ _____

Measurement

Convert to new units.

1. 5 yd = _____ inches

2. 244 in = _____ yd

3. 15 ft = _____ yd

4. 18 yd = _____ ft

5. 12 ft = _____ inches

6. 11 yd = _____ ft

7. 27 ft = _____ yd

8. 30 in = _____ yd

9. 19 yd = _____ ft

1 yd = 36 inch

1 yd = 3 ft

1 ft = 12 inch

1 ft = 0.30 m

10. 9 ft = _____ yd

11. 49 in = _____ yd

12. 64 yd = _____ ft

13. 85 yd = _____ inches

14. 30 ft = _____ yd

15. 20 ft = _____ inches

16. 98 ft = _____ inches

17. 21 ft = _____ yd

18. 10 in = _____ yd

19. Anna 5 feet tall. What is her height in inches?

_____ inches

20. Sara ran 12 yards. What is the distance in feet?

_____ ft

Weights

Convert to new measurements.

1. 5 lb = _____ oz

2. 16 oz = _____ lb

3. 3 lb = _____ oz

4. 20 lb = _____ oz

5. 2 lb = _____ oz

6. 6 lb = _____ oz

7. 32 oz = _____ lb

8. 30 lb = _____ oz

9. 16 lb = _____ oz

1 ton = 2, 000 pounds (lb)

1 lb = 16 ounces (oz)

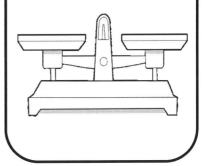

10. 9 lb = _____ oz

11. 12 lb = _____ oz

12. 4 lb = _____ oz

13. 48 oz = _____ lb

14. 60 oz = _____ lb

15. 72 oz = _____ lb

16. 68 oz = _____ lb

17. 56 oz = _____ lb

18. 8 oz = _____ lb

19. If an object weighed 8 lb, how many oz would it weigh?

_____ oz

20. If an object weighed 144 oz, how many lb would it weigh?

_____ lb

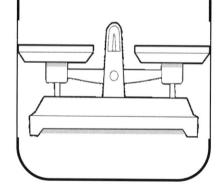

Volume

1. 50 qt = _____ gal

2. 7 gal = _____ qt

3. 4 gal = _____ pt

4. 60 c = _____ qt

5. 14 pt = _____ c

6. 256 c = _____ gal

7. 18 gal = _____ qt

8. 20 gal = _____ pt

9. 6 pt = _____ c

10. 4 pt = _____ qt

✓ 1 Gallons
=
4 Quarts

✓ 1 Quart
=
4 Cups

✓ 1 Gallons
=
16 Cups

✓ 7 Gallons
=
8 Pints

11. 19 qt = _____ pt

12. 13 pt = _____ c

13. 14 gal = _____ qt

14. 20 gal = _____ qt

15. 48 qt = _____ gal

16. 60 c = _____ qt

17. 14 gal = _____ pt

18. 64 c = _____ qt

19. 10 Gallons

=

_____ Quarts

20. 20 Gallons

=

_____ Pints

21. 50 Pints

=

_____ Quarts

22. 70 Cups

=

_____ Pints

Centimeters & Millimeters

1. 10 cm = _____ mm

2. 40 mm = _____ cm

3. 100 cm = _____ mm

4. 60 mm = _____ cm

5. 50 cm = _____ mm

6. 80 mm = _____ cm

7. 20 mm = _____ cm

8. 90 cm = _____ mm

✓ 1 m

=

100 cm

✓ 1 cm

=

10 mm

9. 100 mm = _____ cm

10. 40 cm = _____ mm

11. 30 mm = _____ cm

12. 70 cm = _____ mm

13. 600 cm = _____ mm

14. 1000 mm = _____ cm

15. 80 cm = _____ mm

16. 900 mm = _____ cm

17. 120 mm = _____ cm

18. 110 cm = _____ mm

19. 10 m
=
_____ cm

20. 1000 cm
=
_____ m

21. 12 m
=
_____ cm

22. 2000 cm
=
_____ m

Kilograms & Grams

1. 10 kg = _____ g

2. 33 kg = _____ g

3. 100 kg = _____ g

4. 60 kg = _____ g

5. 85 kg = _____ g

6. 120 kg = _____ g

7. 28 kg = _____ g

8. 72 kg = _____ g

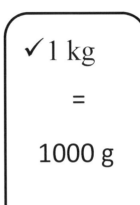

✓ 1 kg

=

1000 g

9. $56 \text{ kg} = $ _____ g

10. $100{,}000 \text{ g} = $ _____ kg

11. $30{,}000 \text{ g} = $ _____ kg

12. $70{,}000 \text{ g} = $ _____ kg

13. $600{,}000 \text{ g} = $ _____ kg

14. $130{,}000 \text{ g} = $ _____ kg

15. $80{,}000 \text{ g} = $ _____ kg

16. $300{,}000 \text{ g} = $ _____ kg

17. $90{,}000 \text{ g} = $ _____ kg

18. $10{,}000 \text{ g} = $ _____ kg

19. 1000 g
    $=$
    _____ kg

20. 3000 g
    $=$
    _____ kg

21. 2 kg
    $=$
    _____ g

22. 4 kg
    $=$
    _____ g

Liters & Milliliters

1. 10 l = _____ ml

2. 4 l = _____ ml

3. 20 l = _____ ml

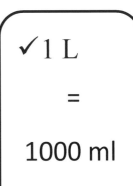

✓ 1 L

=

1000 ml

4. 24 l = _____ ml

5. 27 l = _____ ml

6. 14 l = _____ ml

7. 50 l = _____ ml

8. 45 l = _____ ml

9. 98 l = _____ ml

10. 1000 ml = _____ l

11. 3000 ml = _____ l

12. 70, 000 ml = _____ l

13. 6000 ml = _____ l

14. 13, 000 ml = _____ l

15. 8000 ml = _____ l

16. 30, 000 ml = _____ l

17. 9000 ml = _____ l

18. 10, 000 ml = _____ l

19. 100,000 l = _____ ml

20. 300,000 l = _____ ml

21. 500 ml = _____ l

22. 700 ml = _____ l

Missing Denominator or Numerator

Find the missing values.

1. $\dfrac{1}{2} = \dfrac{}{10}$

6. $\dfrac{9}{27} = \dfrac{}{3}$

2. $\dfrac{}{3} = \dfrac{3}{9}$

7. $\dfrac{2}{28} = \dfrac{4}{}$

3. $\dfrac{}{4} = \dfrac{1}{2}$

8. $\dfrac{5}{18} = \dfrac{15}{}$

4. $\dfrac{6}{12} = \dfrac{1}{}$

9. $\dfrac{6}{12} = \dfrac{}{2}$

5. $\dfrac{}{16} = \dfrac{6}{32}$

10. $\dfrac{2}{10} = \dfrac{}{5}$

11. $\dfrac{6}{18} = \dfrac{2}{}$

16. $\dfrac{3}{24} = \dfrac{1}{}$

12. $\dfrac{}{8} = \dfrac{2}{4}$

17. $\dfrac{}{50} = \dfrac{5}{25}$

13. $\dfrac{12}{\underline{}} = \dfrac{6}{12}$

18. $\dfrac{8}{16} = \dfrac{}{8}$

14. $\dfrac{}{27} = \dfrac{3}{9}$

19. $\dfrac{14}{20} = \dfrac{}{10}$

15. $\dfrac{5}{20} = \dfrac{1}{}$

20. $\dfrac{15}{} = \dfrac{5}{10}$

Roman Numerals

Write in Romans numerals.

1. 2   _____   2. 6   _____

3. 4   _____   4. 9   _____

5. 10   _____   6. 7   _____

7. 3   _____   8. 1   _____

9. 5   _____   10. 8   _____

11. Add 7 + 2 and write in Roman numerals.   _____

12. Add 6 + 5 and write in Roman numerals. _____

13. Subtract 12 – 6 and write in Roman numerals. _____

14. Subtract 20 – 8 and write in Roman numerals. _____

15. Subtract 16 – 9 and write in Roman numerals. _____

16. Add 10 + 10 and write in Roman numerals.   _____

Write in standard numerals.

17. X _____   18. XXX _____

19. L _____   20. LXX _____

21. LXXX _____   22. XL _____

23. XX _____   24. LX _____

25. C _____   26. XC _____

27. Multiply 5 × 5 and write in Roman numerals.

_____

28. find the value of 90 ÷ 5 and write it in Roman numerals.

_____

Simplifying Fractions

Simplify the following fractions.

1. $\dfrac{3}{15} =$

2. $\dfrac{5}{25} =$

3. $\dfrac{10}{30} =$

4. $\dfrac{12}{24} =$

5. $\dfrac{9}{18} =$

6. $\dfrac{4}{16} =$

7. $\dfrac{8}{24} =$

8. $\dfrac{9}{27} =$

9. $\dfrac{2}{30} =$

10. $\dfrac{6}{8} =$

11. $\dfrac{6}{18} =$

12. $\dfrac{15}{30} =$

13. $\dfrac{6}{56} =$

14. $\dfrac{10}{50} =$

15. $\dfrac{30}{45} =$

16. $\dfrac{24}{40} =$

17. $\dfrac{35}{42} =$

18. $\dfrac{15}{45} =$

19. $\dfrac{18}{27} =$

20. $\dfrac{28}{49} =$

21. $\dfrac{48}{54} =$

22. $\dfrac{32}{64} =$

23. $\dfrac{45}{81} =$

24. $\dfrac{27}{54} =$

25. $\dfrac{28}{63} =$

26. $\dfrac{36}{60} =$

Triangles

Write the type of each triangle.

1.

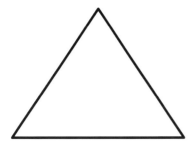

2.

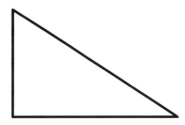

_____

_____

3.

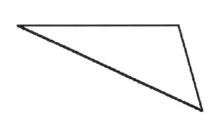

4.

_____

_____

Write scalene, isosceles or equilateral beside each triangle.

5.

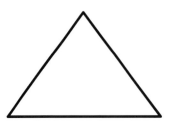

6.

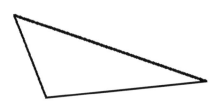

7.

8.

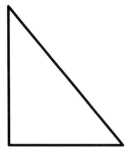

9.

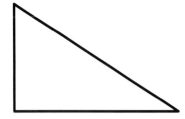

10.

Geometry

Write the names of the following shapes.

1.

2.

3.

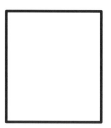

4.

5.

6.

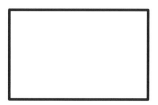

Circle the correct answer.

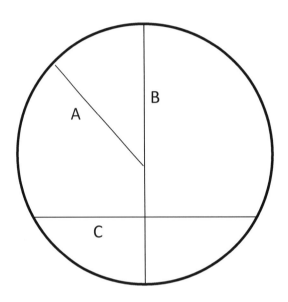

1. A   Diameter   Chord   Radius

2. B   Diameter   Chord   Radius

3. C   Diameter   Chord   Radius

Quadrilaterals

Write the names of the following shapes.

1.
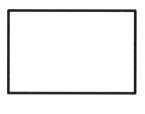

_____

2.
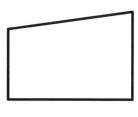

_____

3.
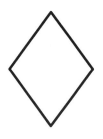

_____

4.

_____

5.
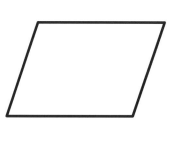

_____

6.

_____

Fill in the blanks.

7. _____ is a shape that has 4 sides and 4 angles.

8. _____ is a quadrilateral that has 2 pairs of parallel sides.

9. _____ is a quadrilateral that has 1 pair of parallel sides.

10. _____ is a parallelogram where all angles are equal

(right angles) and opposite sides are equal.

11. _____ is a parallelogram where opposite angles are

equal and all sides are equal.

12. _____ a parallelogram that is both a rectangle and a

rhombus. It has all right angles and all sides are equal.

Order of Operations

Find the answers.

1. $10 + (14 - 3) = $ _____   2. $(10 + 3) - 9 = $ _____

3. $9 + (12 + 10) = $ _____   4. $14 - (13 - 3) = $ _____

5. $(20 - 6) - 5 = $ _____   6. $(12 + 10) + 5 = $ _____

7. $15 + (17 - 5) = $ _____   8. $19 - (9 + 3) = $ _____

9. $(7 + 8) - 10 = $ _____   10. $(9 - 4) + 18 = $ _____

11. $9 + 12 - (14 - 2) = $ _____

12. $(15 - 5) + 3 + 2 = $ _____

13. $(19 - 2 - 6) + 10 = $ _____

14. $7 + 1 + (17 + 30) = $ _____

Find the answers.

15. $4 \times 5 + (9 - 2) =$ _____

16. $3 + (2 \times 6) =$ _____

17. $(12 + 5) \times (2 - 1) =$ _____

18. $(3 \times 3) - 5 =$ _____

19. $(5 \times 5) + 10 - 3 =$ _____

20. $20 - (4 \times 2) =$ _____

21. $6 \times 3 - (20 - 3) =$ _____

22. $(8 \times 6) - 13 =$ _____

23. $25 + 4 - (4 \times 7) =$ _____

24. $19 + (3 \times 9) =$ _____

25. $22 - 12 - (5 \times 2) =$ _____

26. $(9 \times 6) - 25 =$ _____

27. $(16 - 13) \times (18 - 12) =$ _____

28. $30 - (5 \times 6) =$ _____

29. $10 + 9 - (3 \times 3) =$ _____

30. $(7 \times 8) + 16 =$ _____

Order the Numbers

Arrange the given numbers in descending order.

1. 345, 267, 178, 657   ___, ___, ___, ___

2. 145, 345, 234, 167   ___, ___, ___, ___

3. 890, 786, 986, 678   ___, ___, ___, ___

4. 434, 230, 134, 568   ___, ___, ___, ___

5. 235, 145, 342, 467   ___, ___, ___, ___

6. 156, 223, 467, 134   ___, ___, ___, ___

7. 987, 567, 975, 678   ___, ___, ___, ___

8. 456, 234, 145, 870   ___, ___, ___, ___

Arrange the given numbers in ascending order.

9. 345, 267, 178, 657   ___, ___, ___, ___

10. 145, 345, 234, 167   ___, ___, ___, ___

11. 890, 786, 986, 678   ___, ___, ___, ___

12. 434, 230, 134, 568   ___, ___, ___, ___

13. 235, 145, 342, 467   ___, ___, ___, ___

14. 156, 223, 467, 134   ___, ___, ___, ___

15. 987, 567, 975, 678   ___, ___, ___, ___

16. 456, 234, 145, 870   ___, ___, ___, ___

Improper Fraction

Fill in the blank.

1. $\dfrac{1}{2} + \underline{} = 1$

2. $\dfrac{1}{2} + \underline{} = 4$

3. $\dfrac{2}{3} + \underline{} = 3$

4. $\dfrac{1}{3} + \underline{} = 3$

5. $\dfrac{1}{4} + \underline{} = 1$

6. $\dfrac{6}{9} + \underline{} = 2$

7. $\dfrac{3}{4} + \underline{} = 2$

8. $\dfrac{4}{7} + \underline{} = 2$

9. $\dfrac{3}{5} + \underline{} = 1$

10. $\dfrac{1}{4} + \underline{} = 2$

11. $10 - \underline{\quad} = 5\frac{3}{7}$

12. $3 - \underline{\quad} = 1\frac{1}{2}$

13. $6 - \underline{\quad} = 2\frac{2}{5}$

14. $8 - \underline{\quad} = 3\frac{3}{7}$

15. $5 - \underline{\quad} = 2\frac{1}{5}$

16. $10 - \underline{\quad} = 5\frac{3}{4}$

17. $4 - \underline{\quad} = 2\frac{5}{9}$

18. $8 - \underline{\quad} = 1\frac{1}{10}$

19. $9 - \underline{\quad} = 6\frac{1}{4}$

20. $9 - \underline{\quad} = 4\frac{1}{4}$

Dividing by Tens

Find answers.

1. $300 \div 10 =$ _____　　　　2. $600 \div 20 =$ _____

3. $800 \div 40 =$ _____　　　　4. $450 \div 10 =$ _____

5. $360 \div 60 =$ _____　　　　6. $400 \div 50 =$ _____

7. $450 \div 90 =$ _____　　　　8. $810 \div 90 =$ _____

9. $560 \div 70 =$ _____　　　　10. $280 \div 40 =$ _____

11. $630 \div 70 =$ _____　　　　12. $240 \div 40 =$ _____

13. $350 \div 50 =$ _____　　　　14. $270 \div 30 =$ _____

15. $250 \div 50 =$ _____　　　　16. $180 \div 20 =$ _____

17. $150 \div 30 =$ _____　　　　18. $900 \div 20 =$ _____

19. $\dfrac{320}{10}$

20. $\dfrac{400}{20}$

21. $\dfrac{500}{50}$

22. $\dfrac{210}{30}$

23. $\dfrac{900}{20}$

24. $\dfrac{280}{70}$

25. $\dfrac{360}{60}$

26. $\dfrac{480}{80}$

27. $\dfrac{720}{90}$

28. $\dfrac{640}{80}$

29. $\dfrac{250}{50}$

30. $\dfrac{900}{30}$

31. $\dfrac{150}{30}$

32. $\dfrac{240}{40}$

33. $\dfrac{300}{60}$

34. $\dfrac{450}{90}$

35. $\dfrac{320}{80}$

36. $\dfrac{100}{10}$

Divide 3–Digit Numbers By 1-Digit Numbers

Find the answers.

1. $560 \div 5 =$ _____

2. $120 \div 6 =$ _____

3. $180 \div 3 =$ _____

4. $800 \div 8 =$ _____

5. $540 \div 9 =$ _____

6. $640 \div 8 =$ _____

7. $600 \div 6 =$ _____

8. $900 \div 5 =$ _____

9. $140 \div 7 =$ _____

10. $400 \div 8 =$ _____

11. $100 \div 5 =$ _____

12. $240 \div 4 =$ _____

13. $420 \div 6 =$ _____

14. $560 \div 7 =$ _____

15. $200 \div 4 =$ _____

16. $700 \div 2 =$ _____

17. $450 \div 6 =$ _____

18. $720 \div 5 =$ _____

19. $210 \div 7 =$ _____

20. $300 \div 6 =$ _____

21. $\dfrac{400}{2}$

22. $\dfrac{500}{5}$

23. $\dfrac{800}{5}$

24. $\dfrac{100}{5}$

25. $\dfrac{900}{2}$

26. $\dfrac{300}{3}$

27. $\dfrac{700}{2}$

28. $\dfrac{550}{5}$

29. $\dfrac{950}{5}$

30. $\dfrac{670}{2}$

31. $\dfrac{250}{5}$

32. $\dfrac{220}{5}$

Multiply 1digit By 3–Digit Numbers

Find the answers.

1.
$$\begin{array}{r} 980 \\ \times\ \ 5 \\ \hline \\ \hline \end{array}$$

2.
$$\begin{array}{r} 120 \\ \times\ \ 3 \\ \hline \\ \hline \end{array}$$

3.
$$\begin{array}{r} 240 \\ \times\ \ 4 \\ \hline \\ \hline \end{array}$$

4.
$$\begin{array}{r} 350 \\ \times\ \ 7 \\ \hline \\ \hline \end{array}$$

5.
$$\begin{array}{r} 780 \\ \times\ \ 3 \\ \hline \\ \hline \end{array}$$

6.
$$\begin{array}{r} 632 \\ \times\ \ 8 \\ \hline \\ \hline \end{array}$$

7.
$$\begin{array}{r} 756 \\ \times\ \ 9 \\ \hline \\ \hline \end{array}$$

8.
$$\begin{array}{r} 345 \\ \times\ \ 5 \\ \hline \\ \hline \end{array}$$

9.
$$\begin{array}{r} 289 \\ \times\ \ 9 \\ \hline \\ \hline \end{array}$$

10.
$$\begin{array}{r} 621 \\ \times\ \ 3 \\ \hline \\ \hline \end{array}$$

Find the products.

11. 110 × 2

12. 121 × 3

13. 100 × 4

14. 115 × 6

15. 125 × 2

16. 172 × 5

17. 119 × 8

18. 231 × 3

19. 220 × 2

20. 230 × 5

21. 200 × 9

22. 310 × 2

23. 300 × 4

24. 340 × 2

25. 170 × 7

26. 150 × 5

27. 250 × 2

28. 420 × 3

29. 330 × 3

30. 900 × 2

Comparing Fractions

Use > = < to compare fractions.

1. $\dfrac{1}{4}$ ⬜ $\dfrac{2}{8}$

2. $\dfrac{2}{12}$ ⬜ $\dfrac{1}{2}$

3. $\dfrac{12}{24}$ ⬜ $\dfrac{2}{8}$

4. $\dfrac{4}{10}$ ⬜ $\dfrac{2}{5}$

5. $\dfrac{25}{50}$ ⬜ $\dfrac{1}{2}$

6. $\dfrac{27}{36}$ ⬜ $\dfrac{4}{5}$

7. $\dfrac{6}{18}$ ▢ $\dfrac{10}{30}$ 8. $\dfrac{22}{24}$ ▢ $\dfrac{20}{24}$

9. $\dfrac{1}{2}$ ▢ $\dfrac{1}{2}$ 10. $\dfrac{1}{2}$ ▢ $\dfrac{1}{2}$

11. $\dfrac{3}{6}$ ▢ $\dfrac{24}{48}$ 12. $\dfrac{7}{14}$ ▢ $\dfrac{2}{3}$

Division by Hundred

Find the answers.

1. $500 \div 100 = $ _____

2. $4{,}000 \div 400 = $ _____

3. $1{,}500 \div 500 = $ _____

4. $1{,}800 \div 300 = $ _____

5. $2{,}700 \div 900 = $ _____

6. $800 \div 200 = $ _____

7. $1{,}400 \div 200 = $ _____

8. $2{,}500 \div 500 = $ _____

9. $4,800 \div 600 =$ _____   10. $9,000 \div 200 =$ _____

11. $3,600 \div 600 =$ _____   12. $3,000 \div 500 =$ _____

13. $1,000 \div 200 =$ _____   14. $4,500 \div 900 =$ _____

15. $1,200 \div 600 =$ _____   16. $6,000 \div 200 =$ _____

17. $9,000 \div 300 =$ _____   18. $2,800 \div 400 =$ _____

Missing Numbers

Find the missing numbers.

1. $20 \times \_\_\_ = 60$

7. $\_\_\_ \times 1 = 18$

2. $16 \times \_\_\_ = 32$

8. $21 \times \_\_\_ = 42$

3. $\_\_\_ \times 14 = 84$

9. $20 \times \_\_\_ = 80$

4. $16 \times \_\_\_ = 80$

10. $15 \times 7 = \_\_\_$

5. $\_\_\_ \times 19 = 38$

11. $18 \times 9 = \_\_\_$

6. $17 \times \_\_\_ = 34$

12. $21 \times 4 = \_\_\_$

13. $23 \times 7 =$ ___

20. $21 \times 6 =$ ___

14. ___ $\times 25 = 75$

21. ___ $\times 22 = 154$

15. $24 \times$ ___ $= 120$

22. $19 \times$ ___ $= 76$

16. $22 \times 4 =$ ___

23. $23 \times 9 =$ ___

17. $20 \times$ ___ $= 140$

24. $25 \times 6 =$ ___

18. $17 \times$ ___ $= 153$

25. ___ $\times 18 = 36$

19. ___ $\times 15 = 120$

26. $24 \times$ ___ $= 48$

Triangles And Quadrilaterals

Identify the type of each quadrilateral.

1)

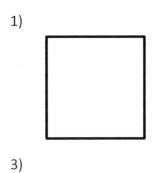

2)

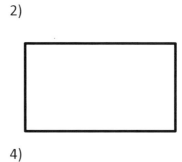

3)

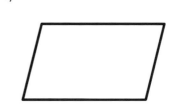

4)

Classify the triangles by their sides and angles.

1)

2)

3)

4)

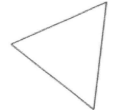

Acute, Obtuse, And Right Triangles

Write the name of the angles.

1)

2)

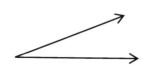

3)

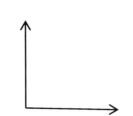

4)

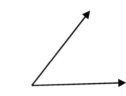

5)

6)

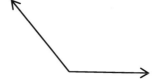

7)

8)

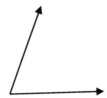

Parallel Sides in Quadrilaterals

Write the name of quadrilaterals.

1)

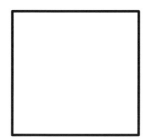

2)

3)

4)

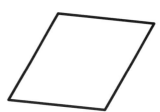

5)

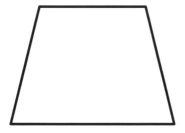

6)

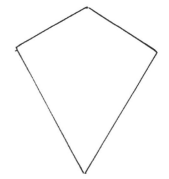

Identify Parallelograms

Write the name of parallelograms.

1)

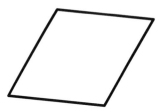

2)

3)

4)

Identify Trapezoids

Which shapes is trapezoid?

1)

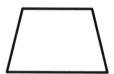

2)

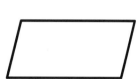

3)

4)

5)

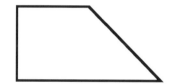

6)

7)

8)

Identify Rectangles

1) A rectangle has _____ sides and _____ angles.

2) Draw a rectangle that is 6 centimeters long and 3 centimeters wide. What is the perimeter?

3) Use a rule and draw a rectangle 5 cm long and 2 cm wide.

4) Draw a rectangle whose length is 4 cm and its width is 2 cm. What is the perimeter of the rectangle?

5) What is the perimeter of the rectangle?

8

4

Identify Rhombuses

Which shape is a Rhombus?

1)

2)

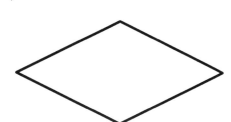

3)

4)

5)

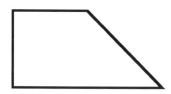

6)

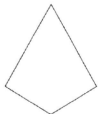

Identify Two–Dimensional Shapes

Write the name of each shape.

1)

2)

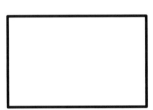

3)

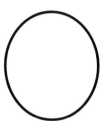

4)

5)

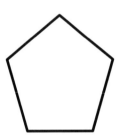

6)

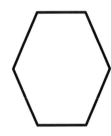

7)

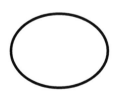

8)

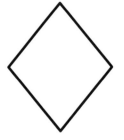

Georgia Milestones Assessment System Practice Test 1

Grade 3

Mathematics

2018

1. Eva had 983 cards. Then, she gave 349 of the cards to her friend Alice. After that, Eva lost 260 cards.

   Which equation can be used to find the number of cards Eve has now?

   A. 983 – 349 + 260 = _____
   B. 983 – 349 – 260 = _____
   C. 983 + 349 + 260 = _____
   D. 983 + 349 – 260 = _____

2. The length of the following rectangle is 7 centimeters and its width is 3 centimeters. What is the area of the rectangle?

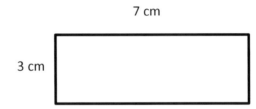

   A. 10 cm^2
   B. 14 cm^2
   C. 20 cm^2
   D. 21 cm^2

3. Which number is made up of 4 hundreds, 8 tens, and 4 ones?
   A. 4084
   B. 484
   C. 448
   D. 844

4. Emily has 108 stickers and she wants to give them to nine of her closest friends. If she gives them all an equal number of stickers, how many stickers will each of Emily's friends receive?

Write your answer in the box below.

5. There are 6 numbers in the box below. Which of the following list shows only odd numbers from the numbers in the box?

15, 30, 42, 18, 83, 29

A. 15, 29, 42
B. 15, 29, 83
C. 15, 30, 42
D. 42, 18, 30

6. Mia's goal is to save $140 to purchase her favorite bike.
    - In January, she saved $36.
    - In February, she saved $28.

    How much money does Mia need to save in March to be able to purchase her favorite bike?

    A. $28
    B. $30
    C. $52
    D. $76

7. Michelle has 72 old books. She plans to send all of them to the library in their area. If she puts the books in boxes which can hold 9 books, which of the following equations can be used to find the number of boxes she will use?

    A. $72 + 9 =$ _____

    B. $72 \times 9 =$ _____

    C. $72 - 9 =$ _____

    D. $72 \div 9 =$ _____

8. Look at the spinner above. On which color is the spinner most likely to land?

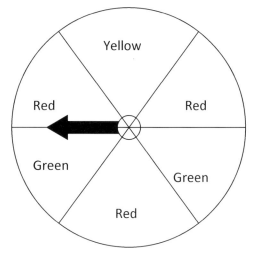

A. Red
B. Green
C. Yellow
D. None

9. A group of third grade students recorded the following distances that they jumped.

23 inches	32 inches	24 inches	28 inches
36 inches	33 inches	25 inches	34 inches
32 inches	28 inches	34 inches	32 inches

What is the distance that was jumped most often?

A. 23
B. 24
C. 32
D. 34

10. A cafeteria menu had spaghetti with meatballs for $8 and bean soup for $6. How much would it cost to buy three plates of spaghetti with meatballs and three bowls of bean soup?

    Write your answer in the box below.

    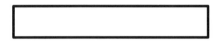

11. The following models are the same size and each divided into equal parts.

    The models can be used to write two fractions.

    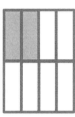 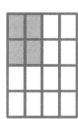

    Based on the models, which of the following statements is true?

    A. $\frac{2}{8}$ is bigger than $\frac{4}{16}$.

    B. $\frac{2}{8}$ is smaller than $\frac{4}{16}$.

    C. $\frac{2}{8}$ is equal to $\frac{4}{16}$.

    D. We cannot compare these two fractions only by using the models.

12. There are 7 days in a week. There are 24 hours in day. How many hours are in a week?
    A. 48
    B. 96
    C. 168
    D. 200

13. Which of the following statements describes the number 24,589?

    A. The sum of two thousands, 4 thousands, five hundreds, eighty tens, and nine ones
    B. The sum of forty thousands, 2 thousands, five hundreds, eight tens, and nine ones
    C. The sum of twenty thousands, 4 thousands, fifty hundreds, eighty tens, and nine ones
    D. The sum of twenty thousands, 4 thousands, five hundreds, eight tens, and nine ones

14. What is the value of "A" in the following equation?

$$21 + A + 9 = 44$$

    A. 10
    B. 12
    C. 14
    D. 20

15. Mr. smith usually eats four meals a day. How many meals does he eat in a week?

    A. 21

    B. 24

    C. 28

    D. 30

16. A football team is buying new uniforms. Each uniform costs $20. The team wants to buy 11 uniforms.

Which equation represents a way to find the total cost of the uniforms?

    A. $(20 \times 10) + (1 \times 11) = 200 + 11$

    B. $(20 \times 10) + (10 \times 1) = 200 + 10$

    C. $(20 \times 10) + (20 \times 1) = 200 + 20$

    D. $(11 \times 10) + (10 \times 20) = 110 + 200$

17. There are 92 students from Lexington Elementary school at the library on Tuesday. The other 54 students in the school are practicing in the classroom. Which number sentence shows the total number of students in Riddle Elementary school?

    A. $92 + 54$

    B. $92 - 54$

    C. 92×54

    D. $92 \div 54$

18. Use the picture below to answer the question.

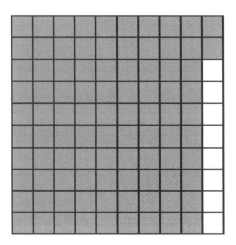

Which fraction shows the shaded part of this square?

A. $\dfrac{92}{100}$

B. $\dfrac{92}{10}$

C. $\dfrac{90}{100}$

D. $\dfrac{8}{100}$

19. Which number correctly completes the number sentence $90 \times 25 = ?$
    A. 225
    B. 900
    C. 1,250
    D. 2,250

20. Which number correctly completes the subtraction sentence
    $8000 - 658 = $ _____ ?

    A. 7,342

    B. 7,452

    C. 742

    D. 7458

21. Jason packs 14 boxes with flashcards. Each box holds 40 flashcards. How many flashcards Jason can pack into these boxes?

    A. 56

    B. 480

    C. 540

    D. 560

22. What is the value of A in the equation 72 ÷ A = 8

    A. 2

    B. 6

    C. 7

    D. 9

23. Use the models below to answer the question.

Which statement about the models is true?

    A. Each shows the same fraction because they are the same size.

    B. Each shows a different fraction because they are different shapes.

    C. Each shows the same fraction because they both have 3 sections shaded.

    D. Each shows a different fraction because they both have 3 shaded sections but a different number of total sections.

24. Emma flew 2,448 miles from Los Angeles to New York City. What is the number of miles Emma flew rounded to the nearest thousand?

   A. 2,000

   B. 2,400

   C. 2,500

   D. 3,000

25. A number sentence such as $31 + Z = 98$ can be called an equation. If this equation is true, then which of the following equations is not true?

   A. $98 - 31 = Z$

   B. $98 - Z = 31$

   C. $Z - 31 = 98$

   D. $Z + 31 = 98$

26. Classroom A contains 8 rows of chairs with 4 chairs per row. If classroom B has three times as many chairs, which number sentence can be used to find the number of chairs in classroom B?

   A. $8 \times 4 + 3$

   B. $8 + 4 \times 3$

   C. $8 \times 4 \times 3$

   D. $8 + 4 + 3$

27. Emily described a number using these clues:

    Three-digit odd numbers that have a 6 in the hundreds place and a 3 in the tens place

    Which number could fit Ella's description?

    A. 627

    B. 637

    C. 632

    D. 636

28. This clock shows a time after 12:00 PM. What time was it 1 hours and 30 minutes ago?

    A. 12:45 PM

    B. 1:45 PM

    C. 1: 15 PM

    D. 12:15 PM

29. Olivia has 84 pastilles. She wants to put them in boxes of 4 pastilles. How many boxes does she need?

    A. 20

    B. 21

    C. 24

    D. 28

30. To what number is the arrow pointing?

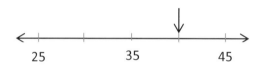

    A. 36

    B. 38

    C. 40

    D. 42

This is the end of the practice test 1

Georgia Milestones Assessment System Practice Test 2

Grade 3

Mathematics

2018

1. Which of the following list shows only fractions that are equivalent to $\frac{1}{3}$?

   A. $\frac{3}{9}, \frac{5}{15}, \frac{24}{72}$

   B. $\frac{6}{12}, \frac{5}{15}, \frac{9}{27}$

   C. $\frac{3}{9}, \frac{4}{15}, \frac{6}{18}$

   D. $\frac{3}{9}, \frac{5}{10}, \frac{8}{24}$

2. What mixed number is shown by the shaded rectangles?

    A. $3\frac{1}{2}$

    B. $4\frac{1}{2}$

    C. 3

    D. 4

3. The perimeter of a square is 24 units. Each side of this square is the same length.

    What is the length of one side of the square in units?

    A. 4

    B. 5

    C. 6

    D. 8

4. There are two different cards on the table.

   - There are 3 rows that have 13 red cards in each row.

   - There are 24 white cards.

   How many cards are there on the table?

   A. 59

   B. 63

   C. 68

   D. 70

5. Which of the following comparison of fractions is true?

   A. $\frac{2}{5} = \frac{4}{10}$

   B. $\frac{2}{5} > \frac{4}{10}$

   C. $\frac{2}{5} < \frac{4}{10}$

   D. $\frac{2}{5} < \frac{2}{10}$

6. The sum of 3 ten thousands, 6 hundreds, and 9 tens can be expressed as what number in standard form?

   A. 3,690

   B. 30,690

   C. 30,069

   D. 30,609

7. What is the perimeter of the following triangle?

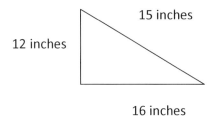

A. 27 inches

B. 31 inches

C. 43 inches

D. 192 inches

8. Which number is represented by A?

$9 \times A = 108$

A. 9

B. 10

C. 11

D. 12

9. What is the perimeter of this rectangle?

8 cm

4 cm

    A. 12 cm

    B. 24 cm

    C. 32 cm

    D. 64 cm

10. Nicole has 4 quarters, 6 dimes, and 5 pennies. How much money does Nicole have?

    A. 155 pennies

    B. 165 pennies

    C. 255 pennies

    D. 265 pennies

11. Michael has 745 marbles. What is this number rounded to the nearest ten?

    Write your answer in the box below.

12. There are 60 minutes in an hour. How many minutes are in 6 hours?

    A. 300 minutes

    B. 320 minutes

    C. 360 minutes

    D. 400 minutes

13. Which number correctly completes the number sentence $55 \times 14 = ?$

    A. 550

    B. 660

    C. 770

    D. 990

14. One side of a square is 4 feet. What is the area of the square?

Write your answer in the box below.

15. Moe has 420 cards. He wants to put them in boxes of 20 cards. How many boxes does he need?

    A. 20
    B. 21
    C. 22
    D. 24

16. There are 9 rows of chairs in a classroom with 6 chairs in each row. How many chairs are in the classroom?
    A. 45
    B. 49
    C. 54
    D. 63

17. What number goes in the box to make the equation true?

$$\frac{\square}{8} = 2$$

    A. 8
    B. 12
    C. 16
    D. 32

18. Use the picture below to answer the question.

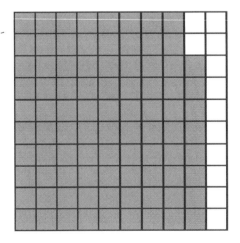

19. Which fraction shows the shaded part of this square?

    A. $\dfrac{88}{100}$

    B. $\dfrac{88}{10}$

    C. $\dfrac{8.8}{100}$

    D. $\dfrac{8}{100}$

20. What number makes this equation true?

$12 \times 8 = \square$

    A. 88
    B. 96
    C. 100
    D. 108

21. Kayla has 109 red cards and 88 white cards. How many more red cards than white cards does Kayla have?

    A. 17
    B. 19
    C. 21
    D. 27

22. A number sentence is shown below.

    $3 \times 7 \,\square\, 6 = 126$

    What symbol goes into the box to make the number sentence true?

    A. $\times$
    B. $\div$
    C. $+$
    D. $-$

23. Liam had 845 marbles. Then, he gave 455 of the cards to his friend Ethan. After that, Liam lost 116 cards.

    Which equation can be used to find the number of cards Eve has now?

    A. $845 - 455 + 116 =$ _____
    B. $845 - 455 - 116 =$ _____
    C. $845 + 455 + 116 =$ _____
    D. $845 + 455 - 116 =$ _____

24. What is the value of "B" in the following equation?

$$33 + B + 8 = 66$$

    A. 16
    B. 18
    C. 22
    D. 25

25. Mason is 18 months now and he usually eats six meals a day. How many meals does he eat in a week?

    A. 36
    B. 40
    C. 42
    D. 48

26. A number sentence such as $66 - x = 18$ can be called an equation. If this equation is true, then which of the following equations is true?

    A. $66 - 18 = x$

    B. $66 - x = 18$

    C. $x - 18 = 66$

    D. $x + 18 = 66 + 18$

27. There are 6 numbers in the box below. Which of the following list shows only even numbers from the numbers in the box?

$$15, 30, 42, 18, 83, 29$$

   A. 15, 29, 42
   B. 15, 29, 83
   C. 15, 30, 42
   D. 42, 18, 30

28. Noah packs 18 boxes with crayons. Each box holds 40 crayons. How many crayons Noah can pack into these boxes?

   A. 480

   B. 540

   C. 680

   D. 720

29. A cafeteria menu had spaghetti with meatballs for $10 and bean soup for $6. How much would it cost to buy three plates of spaghetti with meatballs and two bowls of bean soup?

   Write your answer in the box below.

30. Which number correctly completes the number sentence $25 \times 50 = ?$

    A. 225
    B. 900
    C. 1,250
    D. 2,250

This is the end of practice test 2

GMAS Practice Tests Answer Keys

GMAS Practice Test 1 Answer Key

1.	B	2.	A
3.	C	4.	B
5.	B	6.	D
7.	D	8.	A
9.	C	10.	42
11.	C	12.	C
13.	D	14.	C
15.	C	16.	C
17.	A	18.	A
19.	D	20.	A
21.	D	22.	D
23.	D	24.	A
25.	C	26.	C
27.	B	28.	A
29.	B	30.	C

GMAS Practice Test 2 Answer Key

1.	A	2.	D
3.	64	4.	C
5.	A	6.	B
7.	C	8.	D
9.	B	10.	B
11.	750	12.	C
13.	C	14.	16 feet
15.	B	16.	C
17.	C	18.	C
19.	A	20.	B
21.	C	22.	A
23.	B	24.	D
25.	C	26.	A
27.	D	28.	D
29.	$42	30.	C

Answers of Worksheets

Repeating pattern

1)

2)

3)

4)

5)

6)

7)

8)

Growing patterns

1)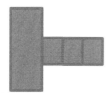

2)

3)

4)

5)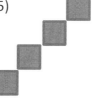

6)

7)

8)

Adding two–digit numbers

1. 58	8. 75	15. 83
2. 36	9. 100	16. 100
3. 51	10. 28	17. 95
4. 24	11. 24	18. 80
5. 73	12. 63	19. 30
6. 49	13. 109	20. 30
7. 96	14. 54	21. 48
22. 60	23. 63	

Subtracting two–digit numbers

1. 27	9. 43	17. 55
2. 38	10. 50	18. 32
3. 60	11. 10	19. 13
4. 8	12. 76	20. 27
5. 53	13. 41	21. 17
6. 69	14. 25	22. 36
7. 57	15. 43	23. 40
8. 51	16. 31	

Adding three–digit numbers

1. 290	9. 1, 045	17. 184
2. 557	10. 275	18. 801
3. 412	11. 528	19. 1,134
4. 580	12. 370	20. 201
5. 862	13. 1,003	21. 765
6. 385	14. 701	22. 590
7. 846	15. 709	23. 396
8. 1, 203	16. 579	

Calendars

1. 5	4. 14th	7. Monday
2. Friday	5. 29th	8. 31 days
3. 11th	6. 11th	

Adding hundreds

1. 400	11. 1000	21. 500
2. 500	12. 800	22. 900
3. 700	13. 700	23. 600
4. 1000	14. 800	24. 900
5. 800	15. 1100	25. 800
6. 600	16. 200	26. 1300
7. 1000	17. 700	27. 1200
8. 900	18. 900	28. 1100
9. 800	19. 600	
10. 400	20. 400	

Round 3–digit numbers

1. 100	9. 600	17. 300
2. 800	10. 300	18. 200
3. 400	11. 900	19. 400
4. 300	12. 500	20. 400
5. 300	13. 300	21. 2000
6. 800	14. 800	22. 7000
7. 900	15. 500	23. 5000
8. 400	16. 400	24. 2000

25. 3000	31. 3000	37. 7000
26. 8000	32. 4000	38. 1000
27. 4000	33. 2000	39. 8000
28. 2000	34. 7000	40. 8000
29. 5000	35. 2000	
30. 9000	36. 3000	

Adding 4–digit numbers

1. 3,500	7. 8, 490	13. 3, 298
2. 2, 900	8. 6, 577	14. 6515
3. 3, 544	9. 8, 454	15. 6291
4. 5, 566	10. 4, 770	16. 9229
5. 3, 084	11. 8, 781	17. 5, 275
6. 6, 891	12. 10, 075	18. 7, 421

Subtracting 4–digit numbers

1. 2, 100		
2. 5, 500	8. 2, 130	14. 3120
3. 1, 114	9. 2, 913	15. 4, 615
4. 4, 663	10. 1, 665	16. 1, 347
5. 4, 545	11. 3, 600	17. 1, 360
6. 3, 840	12. 1, 044	18. 2, 211
7. 1, 785	13. 3, 022	

Estimate sums

1) 70	5) 80	9) 130
2) 80	6) 40	10) 120
3) 90	7) 120	11) 80
4) 70	8) 30	12) 90

13) 110	17) 190	21) 160
14) 120	18) 120	22) 130
15) 780	19) 150	23) 110
16) 120	20) 70	24) 110

Estimate differences

1) 40	9) 40	17) 20
2) 0	10) 20	18) 20
3) 30	11) 40	19) 10
4) 10	12) 40	20) 60
5) 20	13) 30	21) 10
6) 20	14) 20	22) 60
7) 30	15) 30	23) 80
8) 20	16) 30	24) 50

Estimate products

1) 600	9) 200	17) 3600
2) 200	10) 3200	18) 900
3) 600	11) 1500	19) 1600
4) 800	12) 700	20) 4500
5) 1400	13) 1000	21) 6300
6) 3600	14) 4200	22) 1600
7) 4500	15) 4500	23) 500
8) 800	16) 2800	24) 6000

Fractions

1.

2.

3.

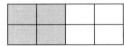

4.

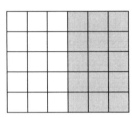

5.

6.

7.

8.

Fractions of a number

1) 20	4) 12	7) 9
2) 60	5) 2	8) 20
3) 25	6) 12	9) 2

10) 9	14) 3	18) 128
11) 25	15) 99	19) 28
12) 28	16) 54	20) 24
13) 10	17) 300	

Order fractions

1) $\dfrac{2}{3}, \dfrac{1}{2}, \dfrac{1}{4}$

8) $\dfrac{9}{8}, \dfrac{5}{8}, \dfrac{3}{8}$

15) $\dfrac{1}{7}, \dfrac{3}{7}, \dfrac{5}{7}$

2) $\dfrac{7}{10}, \dfrac{1}{2}, \dfrac{1}{10}$

9) $\dfrac{4}{5}, \dfrac{3}{5}, \dfrac{2}{5}$

16) $\dfrac{3}{2}, \dfrac{5}{2}, \dfrac{9}{2}$

3) $\dfrac{5}{8}, \dfrac{3}{10}, \dfrac{1}{10}$

10) $\dfrac{8}{3}, \dfrac{5}{3}, \dfrac{1}{3}$

17) $\dfrac{2}{3}, \dfrac{8}{3}, \dfrac{11}{3}$

4) $\dfrac{3}{4}, \dfrac{4}{7}, \dfrac{3}{8}$

11) $\dfrac{5}{3}, \dfrac{7}{3}, \dfrac{8}{3}$

18) $\dfrac{18}{5}, \dfrac{19}{5}, \dfrac{22}{5}$

5) $\dfrac{7}{10}, \dfrac{3}{8}, \dfrac{1}{3}$

12) $\dfrac{4}{9}, \dfrac{5}{9}, \dfrac{8}{9}$

19) $\dfrac{4}{13}, \dfrac{8}{13}, \dfrac{12}{13}$

6) $\dfrac{1}{2}, \dfrac{3}{8}, \dfrac{1}{8}$

13) $\dfrac{1}{8}, \dfrac{3}{8}, \dfrac{5}{8}$

20) $\dfrac{3}{20}, \dfrac{11}{20}, \dfrac{18}{20}$

7) $\dfrac{1}{2}, \dfrac{2}{5}, \dfrac{1}{5}$

14) $\dfrac{1}{4}, \dfrac{2}{4}, \dfrac{3}{4}$

Value of "x"

1. 2	9. 1	17. 27
2. 2	10. 20	18. 5
3. 6	11. 4	19. 16
4. 3	12. 8	20. 2
5. 8	13. 14	21. 35
6. 7	14. 4	22. 4
7. 5	15. 4	23. 5
8. 8	16. 32	24. 47

Comparing

1. $35 < 67$	15. 23 less than 34
2. $89 > 56$	16. 89 less than 98
3. $56 > 35$	17. 45 greater than 25
4. $27 < 56$	18. 34 greater than 32
5. $34 = 34$	19. 91 equal to 91
6. $28 < 45$	20. 57 greater than 55
7. $89 > 67$	21. 85 greater than 78
8. $90 > 56$	22. 56 greater than 43
9. $94 < 98$	23. 34 equal to 34
10. $48 > 23$	24. 92 less than 98
11. $24 < 54$	25. 38 less than 46
12. $89 = 89$	26. 67 greater than 58
13. $50 > 30$	27. 88 greater than 69
14. $20 = 20$	28. 23 less than 34

Adding decimal numbers

1. 7	7. 15.1	13. 10.7
2. 3	8. 6.9	14. 11.4
3. 11.8	9. 17.9	15. 9
4. 10.3	10. 8.3	16. 5.2
5. 10.7	11. 8.6	17. 7.9
6. 7.9	12. 12.8	18. 8.3

Positions

1. Inside	4. Under	7. Left
2. top	5. Right	8. Right
3. at the side	6. Middle	9. Left

Read clocks

1. 1	3. 4	5. 10 : 15
2. 5 : 45	4. 3 : 30	6. 8 : 35

Electronic Clock

1. It's two thirty.
2. It's three Fifteen.
3. It's five forty–five.
4. It's nine twenty.
5. It's ten five.
6. It's Twelve Fifty.
7. It's ten Twenty–five.
8. It's three Twenty–three.
9. It's Eleven fifty seven.
10. It's two Twelve.
11. It's one two.
12. It's eight thirty five.
13. It's six× forty six×.

Multiplication by 0, 1, 2 , 3

1. 18
2. 28
3. 30
4. 0
5. 12
6. 15
7. 72
8. 30
9. 22
10. 36
11. 39
12. 9
13. 8
14. 2
15. 3
16. 21
17. 3
18. 4
19. 2
20. 3
21. 30
22. 0
23. 9
24. 1
25. 3
26. 21

Multiplication by 4, 5, 6

1. 40
2. 48
3. 45
4. 28
5. 32
6. 54
7. 36
8. 84
9. 72
10. 66
11. 48
12. $6 \times 6 = 36$
13. $11 \times 4 = 44$
14. $9 \times 5 = 45$
15. $12 \times 6 = 72$
16. $15 \times 5 = 75$

Multiplication by 7, 8, 9

1. 49
2. 72
3. 54
4. 70
5. 88
6. 63
7. 108
8. 64
9. 81
10. 77
11. 96
12. 56
13. 0
14. 9
15. 8
16. 7
17. 9
18. 5

19. 10	24. 56	29. 9
20. 5	25. 1	30. 81
21. 8	26. 72	31. 72
22. 2	27. 16	
23. 2	28. 10	

Multiplication by 10, 11, 12

1. 66	11. 80	21. 1
2. 96	12. 120	22. 8
3. 60	13. 132	23. 1
4. 33	14. 8	24. 7
5. 108	15. 8	25. 66
6. 40	16. 36	26. 4
7. 88	17. 6	27. 55
8. 60	18. 9	28. 168
9. 90	19. 108	29. 150
10. 144	20. 72	

Division by 0, 1, 2, 3

1. 2	7. 12	13. 2
2. 8	8. 9	14. 7
3. 6	9. 16	15. 3
4. 12	10. 18	16. 21
5. 9	11. 2	17. 10
6. 5	12. 1	

18. $4 \times 2 = 8$, $8 \div 2 = 4$
19. $8 \times 3 = 24$, $24 \div 3 = 8$
20. $10 \times 2 = 20$, $20 \div 2 = 10$
21. $6 \times 3 = 18$, $18 \div 3 = 6$
22. $12 \times 2 = 24$, $24 \div 2 = 12$
23. 10
24. 5
25. 9
26. 9

Division by 4, 5, 6

1. 6	10. 6	19. 2
2. 6	11. 6	20. 54
3. 5	12. 4	21. 8
4. 4	13. 4	22. $36 \div 6 = 6$
5. 5	14. 42	23. $35 \div 5 = 7$
6. 5	15. 4	24. $40 \div 4 = 10$
7. 18	16. 2	25. $42 \div 6 = 7$
8. 6	17. 20	26. $40 \div 5 = 8$
9. 12	18. 8	

Division by 7, 8, 9

1. 8	8. 72	15. 9
2. 21	9. 9	16. 9
3. 11	10. 5	17. 10
4. 7	11. 63	18. 7
5. 8	12. 9	19. 8
6. 81	13. 7	
7. 7	14. 2	

20. 20. $9 \times 4 = 36$, $36 \div 9 = 4$
21. 21. $7 \times 8 = 56$, $56 \div 7 = 8$
22. $9 \times 8 = 72$, $72 \div 8 = 9$
23. 23. $6 \times 8 = 48$, $48 \div 8 = 6$
24. 24. $8 \times 5 = 40$, $40 \div 8 = 5$
25. $8 \times 8 = 64$
26. $9 \times 8 = 72$

Division by 10, 11, 12

1. 10	11. 88	21. 6
2. 4	12. 132	22. 8
3. 11	13. 10	23. 9
4. 7	14. 132	24. 9
5. 11	15. 7	25. 8
6. 12	16. 8	26. 3
7. 40	17. 1	27. 12
8. 10	18. 12	28. 10
9. 12	19. 10	29. 6
10. 10	20. 9	30. 2

Measurement

1. 5 yd = 180 in
2. 244 in = 7 yd
3. 15 ft = 5 yd
4. 18 yd = 648 ft
5. 12 ft = 144 in
6. 11 yd = 33 ft
7. 27 ft = 9 yd
8. 30 in = 0.833 yd
9. 19 yd = 57 ft
10. 9 ft = 3 yd
11. 49 in = 1.36 yd
12. 64 yd = 192 ft
13. 85 yd = 3060 in
14. 30 ft = 10 yd
15. 20 ft = 240 in
16. 98 ft = 1176 in
17. 21 ft = 7 yd
18. 10 in = 0.27 yd
19. 60 in
20. 36 ft

Weights

1. 5 lb = 240oz
2. 16 oz = 1 lb
3. 3 lb = 48oz
4. 20 lb = 320 oz
5. 2 lb = 32 oz
6. 6 lb = 96 oz
7. 15 oz = 0.937 lb
8. 30 lb = 480 oz
9. 16 lb = 256 oz
10. 9 lb = 144 oz
11. 12 lb = 192 oz
12. 4 lb = 64 oz
13. 20 oz = 1.25lb
14. 30 oz = 1.875 lb
15. 26 oz = 1.625 lb
16. 10 oz = 0.625 lb
17. 21 oz = 1.312 lb
18. 11 oz = 0.687 lb
19. 64
20. 9

Volumes

1. 50 qt = 12.5 gal
2. 7 gal = 28 qt
3. 4 gal = 32 pt
4. 60 c = 15 qt
5. 14 pt = 96 c
6. 256 c = 16 gal

7. 18 gal = 72 qt

8. 20 gal = 160 pt

9. 6 pt = 12 c

10. 4 pt = 2 qt

11. 19 qt = 38 pt

12. 13 pt = 26 c

13. 14 gal = 56 qt

14. 20 gal = 80 qt

15. 48 qt = 12 gal

16. 60 c = 15 qt

17. 14 gal = 112 pt

18. 64 c = 16 qt

19. 10 Gallons = 40 Quarts

20. 20 Gallons =160 Pints

21. 50 Pints =25 Quarts

22. 70 Cups =35 Pints

Centimeters & Millimeters

1. 10 cm = 100 mm

2. 40 mm = 4 cm

3. 100 cm = 1000 mm

4. 60 mm = 6 cm

5. 50 cm = 500 mm

6. 80 mm = 8 cm

7. 20 mm = 2 cm

8. 90 cm = 900 mm

9. 100 mm = 10 cm

10. 40 cm = 400 mm

11. 30 mm = 3 cm

12. 70 cm = 700 mm

13. 600 cm = 6000 mm

14. 1000 mm = 100 cm

15. 80 cm = 800 mm

16. 900 mm = 90 cm

17. 120 mm = 12 cm

18. 110 cm = 1100 mm

19. 10 m = 1000 cm

20. 1000 cm = 10 m

21. 12 m = 12 cm

22. 2000 cm = 20

Kilograms & Grams

1. 10 kg = 10000 g

2. 33 kg = 33000 g

3. 100 kg = 100000 g

4. 60 kg = 60000 g

5. 85 kg = 85000 g

6. 120 kg = 120000g

7. 28 kg = 28000 g

8. 72 kg = 72000 g

9. 56 kg = 5600 g

10. 100,000 g = 100 kg

11. 30, 000 g = 30 kg

12. 70, 000 g = 70 kg

13. 600, 000 g = 600 kg

14. 130, 000 g = 130 kg

15. 80,000 g = 80 kg

16. 300, 000 g = 300 kg

17. 90, 000 g = 90 kg

18. 10, 000 g = 10 kg

19. 1 kg

20. 3 kg

21. 2000 g

22. 4000 g

Liters & Milliliters

1. 10 l = 1000 ml

2. 4 l = 4000 ml

3. 20 l = 20000 ml

4. 24 l = 24000 ml

5. 27 l = 27000 ml

6. 14 l = 14000 ml

7. 50 l = 50000 ml

8. 45 l = 45000 ml

9. 98 l = 98000 ml

10. 1000 ml = 1 l

11. 3000 ml = 3 l

12. 70, 000 ml = 70 l

13. 6000 ml = 6 l

14. 13, 000 ml = 13 l

15. 8000 ml = 8 l

16. 30, 000 ml = 30 l

17. 9000 ml = 9 l

18. 10, 000 ml = 10 l

19. 100

20. 300

21. 500,000

22. 700,000

Missing Denominator

1. 5
2. 1
3. 2
4. 2
5. 3
6. 1
7. 56

8. 54
9. 1
10. 1
11. 6
12. 4
13. 24
14. 9

15. 4
16. 8
17. 10
18. 4
19. 7
20. 30

Roman Numerals

1. II
2. VI
3. IV
4. IX
5. X
6. VII
7. III

8. I
9. V
10. VIII
11. IX
12. XI
13. VI
14. XII

15. VII
16. XX
17. 10
18. 30
19. 50
20. 70
21. 80

22. 40
23. 20
24. 60

25. 100
26. 90
27. XXV

28. XXVII

Simplifying Fractions

1. $\frac{1}{5}$

2. $\frac{1}{5}$

3. $\frac{1}{3}$

4. $\frac{1}{2}$

5. $\frac{1}{2}$

6. $\frac{1}{4}$

7. $\frac{1}{3}$

8. $\frac{1}{3}$

9. $\frac{1}{15}$

10. $\frac{3}{4}$

11. $\frac{1}{3}$

12. $\frac{1}{2}$

13. $\frac{3}{28}$

14. $\frac{1}{5}$

15. $\frac{2}{3}$

16. $\frac{3}{5}$

17. $\frac{5}{6}$

18. $\frac{1}{3}$

19. $\frac{2}{3}$

20. $\frac{4}{7}$

21. $\frac{2}{3}$

22. $\frac{1}{2}$

23. $\frac{5}{9}$

24. $\frac{1}{3}$

25. $\frac{4}{9}$

26. $\frac{3}{5}$

Triangles

1. equilateral

2. scalene

3. scalene

4. isosceles triangle

5. equilateral triangle

6. scalene triangle

7. isosceles

8. right triangle

9. right triangle

10. equilateral triangle

Geometry

1. regular pentagon	5. rectangle
2. parallelogram	6. radius
3. square	7. diameter
4. triangle	8. chord

Quadrilaterals

1. Rectangle	7. Quadrilateral
2. Trapezoid	8. Parallelogram
3. Rhombus	9. Trapezoid
4. Square	10. Rectangle
5. Parallelogram	11. Rhombus
6. Trapezoid	12. Square

Order of Operations

1. 21	11. 9	21. 1
2. 4	12. 15	22. 35
3. 31	13. 21	23. 1
4. 4	14. 55	24. 46
5. 19	15. 27	25. 0
6. 27	16. 15	26. 29
7. 27	17. 17	27. 12
8. 7	18. 4	28. 0
9. 5	19. 18	29. 10
10. 23	20. 12	30. 72

Order the Numbers

1. 657, 345, 267, 178
2. 345, 234, 167, 145
3. 986, 890, 786, 678
4. 568, 434, 230, 134
5. 467, 342, 235, 145
6. 467, 223, 156, 134
7. 987, 975, 678, 567
8. 870, 456, 234, 145

9. 178, 267, 345, 657
10. 145, 167, 234, 345
11. 678, 786, 890, 986
12. 134, 230, 434, 568
13. 145, 235, 342, 467
14. 134, 156, 223, 467
15. 567, 678, 975, 987
16. 145, 234, 456, 870

Improper Fraction

1. $\frac{1}{2}$
2. $3\frac{1}{2}$
3. $\frac{7}{3}$
4. $\frac{8}{3}$

5. $\frac{3}{4}$
6. $\frac{12}{9}$
7. $\frac{5}{4}$
8. $\frac{10}{7}$

9. $\frac{2}{5}$
10. $\frac{7}{4}$

Dividing by tens

1. 30
2. 30
3. 20
4. 45
5. 6
6. 8
7. 5
8. 9
9. 8
10. 7
11. 9
12. 6

13. 7
14. 9
15. 5
16. 9
17. 5
18. 45
19. 32
20. 20
21. 10
22. 7
23. 45
24. 4

25. 6
26. 6
27. 8
28. 8
29. 5
30. 3
31. 5
32. 6
33. 5
34. 5
35. 4
36. 10

Divide 3 digit numbers by 1 digit numbers

1. 112
2. 60
3. 60
4. 100
5. 60
6. 80
7. 100
8. 180
9. 70
10. 50
11. 20
12. 60
13. 70
14. 80
15. 50
16. 140
17. 75
18. 144
19. 30
20. 50
21. 200
22. 100
23. 40
24. 20
25. 450
26. 100
27. 350
28. 110
29. 190
30. 335
31. 50
32. 44

Multiply 1digit by 3 digit

1. 4,900
2. 40
3. 960
4. 2,450
5. 2,340
6. 5,056
7. 6,804
8. 1,725
9. 2,601
10. 1,863
11. 220
12. 363
13. 400
14. 690
15. 250
16. 860
17. 952
18. 693
19. 440
20. 1150
21. 1800
22. 620
23. 1200
24. 680
25. 1190
26. 750
27. 500
28. 1260
29. 990
30. 1800

Comparing fractions

1. $\frac{1}{4} = \frac{2}{8}$
2. $\frac{2}{12} < \frac{1}{2}$
3. $\frac{12}{24} > \frac{2}{8}$
4. $\frac{4}{10} = \frac{2}{5}$
5. $\frac{25}{50} = \frac{1}{2}$
6. $\frac{27}{36} < \frac{4}{5}$
7. $\frac{6}{18} = \frac{10}{30}$
8. $\frac{22}{24} > \frac{20}{24}$
9. $\frac{1}{2} = \frac{1}{2}$
10. $\frac{1}{2} = \frac{1}{2}$
11. $\frac{3}{6} = \frac{24}{48}$
12. $\frac{7}{14} < \frac{2}{3}$

Division by Hundred

1. 5	7. 7	13. 5
2. 10	8. 5	14. 5
3. 3	9. 8	15. 2
4. 6	10. 45	16. 30
5. 3	11. 6	17. 3
6. 4	12. 6	18. 7

Missing Numbers

1. 3	10. 105	19. 8
2. 2	11. 162	20. 126
3. 6	12. 84	21. 7
4. 5	13. 161	22. 4
5. 2	14. 3	23. 207
6. 2	15. 5	24. 150
7. 18	16. 88	25. 2
8. 2	17. 7	26. 2
9. 4	18. 9	

Triangles and quadrilaterals

1) Square
2) Rectangle
3) Trapezoid
4) Parallelogram
5) Scalene, obtuse
6) Isosceles, right
7) Scalene, right
8) Equilateral, acute

Acute, obtuse, and right triangles

1) Obtuse
2) Acute
3) Right
4) Acute
5) Straight
6) Obtuse
7) Obtuse
8) Acute

Parallel Sides in Quadrilaterals

1) Square   3) Parallelogram   5) Trapezoid

2) Rectangle   4) Rhombus   6) Kike

Identify Parallelograms

1) Rhombus   3) Rectangles

2) Squares   4) Parallelogram

Identify Trapezoids

Number of 1, 4, 5, 7

Identify Rhombuses

Number of 2

Identify two–dimensional shapes

1) Triangle   5) Pentagon

2) Rectangle   6) Hexagon

3) Circle   7) Oval

4) Square   8) diamond

"Effortless Math Education" Publications

Effortless Math Education authors' team strives to prepare and publish the best quality Mathematics learning resources to make learning Math easier for all. We hope that our publications help you or your student learn Math in an effective way.

We all in Effortless Math wish you good luck and successful studies!

Effortless Math Authors

Online Math Lessons

Enjoy interactive Math lessons online

with the best Math teachers

Online Math learning that's effective, affordable, flexible, and fun

Learn Math wherever you want; when you want

Ultimate flexibility. You can now learn Math online, enjoy high quality engaging lessons no matter where in the world you are. It's affordable too.

Learn Math with one-on-one classes

We provide one-on-one Math tutoring online. We believe that one-to-one tutoring is the most effective way to learn Math.

Qualified Math tutors

Working with the best Math tutors in the world is the key to success! Our tutors give you the support and motivation you need to succeed with a personal touch.

Online Math Lessons

It's easy! Here's how it works.

1- Request a FREE introductory session.

2- Meet a Math tutor online.

3- Start Learning Math in Minutes.

Send Email to: info@EffortlessMath.com

Or Call: +1-469-230-3605

Made in the USA
Middletown, DE
27 February 2023

25770953R00097